THE LEGENDS OF THE PUNJABI WARRIORS

The Sikh Warriors Of Punjab

BY

ROMAN SIDHU

THE LEGENDS OF THE PUNJABI WARRIORS : THE SIKH WARRIORS OF PUNJAB

ISBN :- 9798395518408

Printed in the India by SARDARGARH INC (www.Sardargarhinc.blogspot.com)

Dedication

Dedicated to the land of five rivers, Punjab, and its vibrant culture that has inspired me to pen down this book. This work is dedicated to all the Punjabis who have kept their heritage alive through their love for their roots, their language, their music, and their food. May this book serve as a small tribute to the rich history, traditions, and values of Punjab, and its people who have contributed so much to the world. Thank you for the inspiration and the opportunity to share this amazing culture with the world.

Phone: 94632-31564

Email: SARDARGARHinc@gmail.com

Online   Chat: go   to   our   website: **www.Sardargarhinc.blogspot.com**[1].

---

1.   http://www.sardargarhinc.blogspot.com

Foreword

It gives me great pleasure to write the foreword for this book, Legends of the Punjabi Warriors, by Roman Sidhu. As someone who has spent years studying and researching the history of Punjab, I can say that this book is a valuable addition to the literature on Punjab's rich cultural heritage.

Through this book, Roman Sidhu has done an excellent job of bringing to life the tales of some of the greatest warriors of Punjab. The book takes the reader on a journey through time, exploring the lives of legendary warriors like Banda Singh Bahadur, Maharaja Ranjit Singh, and Shaheed Bhagat Singh.

What I particularly appreciate about this book is how Roman has contextualized these legends within the broader historical and cultural landscape of Punjab. He provides the reader with a deep understanding of the socio-political conditions that gave rise to these warriors and the impact they had on the society and the culture of Punjab.

Another strength of this book is the way Roman has woven together various sources, including historical accounts, folktales, and ballads, to create a compelling narrative. The stories are told in a way that is engaging and accessible to readers of all ages.

In conclusion, I highly recommend this book to anyone interested in learning more about the history and culture of Punjab. The legends of these warriors have been an inspiration to many generations of Punjabis, and through this book, their legacy will continue to live on.

Dr. Jaspal Singh, Professor of History, Punjabi University, Patiala

Preface

Punjab, a land of brave hearts and fierce warriors, has a rich history of valour and bravery. From the legendary warrior-king Maharaja Ranjit Singh to the gallant freedom fighters of the 20th century, Punjab has produced some of the finest warriors the world has ever seen.

This book, Legends of the Punjabi Warriors, is an attempt to bring to light the tales of some of the greatest warriors of Punjab. It is a tribute to their courage, strength, and determination in the face of adversity. These are stories of warriors who never backed down, even in the face of death, and who fought for what they believed in.

Through these legends, we hope to honour the memory of these great warriors and inspire future generations to learn from their example. We also hope to showcase the rich cultural heritage of Punjab, which has produced a long line of fearless warriors.

The book is not just a collection of stories, but also a journey into the heart of Punjab, its culture, its people, and its history. We hope that readers will find these stories as inspiring and captivating as we did while writing them.

We extend our heartfelt gratitude to all those who have contributed to the making of this book. It is our hope that this book will help keep the legacy of Punjab's warriors alive for generations to come.

Introduction

Deep in the heart of Punjab, there existed a dream. A dream to create a team that would make the people proud, that would inspire future generations, and that would leave an indelible mark on the history of the region. This dream was shared by a group of passionate individuals, who poured their hearts and souls into bringing it to life.

It was a daunting task, fraught with challenges at every turn. But these warriors were undaunted, and they pressed on with a fierce determination that knew no bounds. They scoured the land for the best talent, assembled a team of champions, and set out to conquer the world.

Their journey was marked by triumphs and setbacks, joy and pain, but through it all, they never lost sight of their ultimate goal. With every victory, they grew stronger, and with every defeat, they learned valuable lessons that they would use to fuel their future success.

And so, the Punjab Warriors were born, a force to be reckoned with, a symbol of hope and resilience for all who dared to dream. Their story is one of perseverance, of passion, and of unbridled determination in the face of adversity. And it is a story that will be told for generations to come.

Chapter One : The Sikhs

In the early 16th century, a new religious movement emerged in India that would forever change the course of history. This movement, known as Sikhism, was founded by Guru Nanak Dev Ji, a visionary who sought to bridge the gap between the Hindu and Muslim communities of his time.

Over the years, Sikhism grew in popularity and influence, attracting followers from all walks of life. The Sikhs, as they came to be known, were known for their bravery, their devotion, and their unflinching commitment to justice and equality.

It is in this context that our story begins, in the lush green fields of Punjab, where a young Sikh boy named Jaspal Singh was born. From an early age, Jaspal showed great promise, both as a student and as an athlete. He was deeply committed to his faith, and spent many hours studying the teachings of the Guru Granth Sahib, the holy book of Sikhism.

As he grew older, Jaspal became increasingly aware of the challenges facing his community. The Sikhs were a minority in a predominantly Hindu and Muslim country, and often faced discrimination and persecution as a result. Jaspal was determined to do something about this, to stand up for his people and to fight for their rights.

It was this determination that led him to the world of field hockey, a sport that had long been dominated by Western countries. Jaspal saw an opportunity to use hockey as a way to showcase the talent and resilience of the Sikh community, and to inspire other young Sikhs to pursue their dreams, no matter the odds.

And so, Jaspal began to train in earnest, honing his skills and building his strength. He faced many challenges along the way, from financial difficulties to social stigma, but he persevered, driven by a fierce sense of purpose and a deep love for his community.

As Jaspal's talent and reputation grew, he began to attract the attention of other young Sikh athletes, who saw in him a role model and a leader. Together, they formed a team, the Punjab Warriors, and set out to take the field hockey world by storm.

It was the beginning of a remarkable journey, one that would see the Punjab Warriors rise to greatness, and leave an indelible mark on the history of both Sikhism and field hockey.

1.1 History of Sikhs

The history of Sikhism can be traced back to the early 16th century, when Guru Nanak Dev Ji, the founder of the religion, began spreading his teachings in the region of Punjab, which is now split between India and Pakistan.

Guru Nanak was born in 1469 in a small village in Punjab, and from a young age, he showed a deep interest in spirituality and meditation. He was deeply disturbed by the religious and social divisions he saw around him, and he began to preach a message of unity and love for all.

Over the years, Guru Nanak traveled extensively throughout the region, spreading his message and attracting followers from all walks of life. He was followed by nine other gurus, each of whom contributed to the growth and development of the Sikh faith.

Under the guidance of the gurus, Sikhism grew into a major religious and cultural force in Punjab. The Sikhs were known for their bravery, their commitment to justice and equality, and their devotion to the teachings of the Guru Granth Sahib, the holy book of Sikhism.

However, the history of the Sikhs was not without its challenges. The Sikhs were a minority in a predominantly Hindu and Muslim country, and often faced discrimination and persecution as a result. They were subject to heavy taxes, forced conversions, and other forms of oppression.

Despite these challenges, the Sikhs continued to grow in number and influence, and played an important role in shaping the history and culture of Punjab. They were known for their martial skills, and were often called upon to defend their communities against outside threats.

Today, Sikhism is one of the world's major religions, with millions of followers around the globe. Its teachings of equality, social justice, and devotion to the divine continue to inspire people of all backgrounds and beliefs.

1.2 The Beginning Of Sikh Warriors

The father of Guru Gobind Singh, Guru Tegh Bahadur, was a spiritual leader who played a pivotal role in shaping his son's life and teachings. Guru Tegh Bahadur was the ninth Sikh Guru and was known for his devotion to God and his commitment to fighting against oppression and tyranny.

As a young boy, Guru Gobind Singh was greatly influenced by his father's teachings and his example. He saw firsthand how his father stood up against the tyranny of the Mughal Empire and fought for the rights of the people. Guru Tegh Bahadur's death at the hands of the Mughals, who had ordered him to convert to Islam, left a profound impact on Guru Gobind Singh's life and teachings.

Guru Gobind Singh was only nine years old when his father was executed, and his upbringing was greatly influenced by his father's martyrdom. He saw the sacrifices that his father had made for his faith and his people, and this influenced him greatly in his later life. He was determined to continue his father's legacy and fight against tyranny and injustice.

Guru Gobind Singh's teachings were greatly influenced by his father's legacy. He believed in the power of God and the importance of standing up for what is right. He founded the Khalsa, a community of devout Sikhs who followed a strict code of conduct and who were dedicated to fighting for justice and freedom. The Khalsa was created as a means of resistance to the Mughal Empire, and it played a critical role in liberating the people of Punjab from oppression.

Guru Gobind Singh's life and teachings are a testament to the enduring legacy of his father, Guru Tegh Bahadur. They are an embodiment of the courage, determination, and faith that were instilled in him from a young age. Guru Gobind Singh's teachings continue to inspire people around the world to stand up against oppression and injustice, and to fight for what is right.

The father-son relationship between Guru Tegh Bahadur and Guru Gobind Singh is a shining example of the power of faith and the importance of standing up for what is right, even in the face of great adversity.

Sri Guru Gobind Singh is one of the most revered figures in Sikh history, and his life was marked by extraordinary courage, leadership, and devotion. He was the tenth and the last Sikh Guru, who played a pivotal role in shaping the Sikh faith and its traditions.

Guru Gobind Singh was born in Patna, India, in 1666, and was the only son of Guru Tegh Bahadur, the ninth Sikh Guru. He was educated in several languages and was trained in martial arts and warfare, which later helped him in leading his followers against oppression and tyranny.

At the young age of nine, Guru Gobind Singh became the tenth Sikh Guru after the martyrdom of his father. He was a visionary leader who dedicated his life to the betterment of his people. He wrote many works of poetry and literature, including the Dasam Granth, which is considered one of the most significant works of literature in the Sikh tradition.

Guru Gobind Singh was a fierce warrior who fought against the oppression of the Mughal Empire, which had oppressed the local population for centuries. He founded the Khalsa, a community of devout Sikhs who followed a strict code of conduct, and who were dedicated to fighting for justice and freedom. The Khalsa was created as a means of resistance to the Mughal empire, and it played a critical role in liberating the people of Punjab from oppression.

Guru Gobind Singh was a master of diplomacy and a skilled strategist. He forged alliances with other communities and kingdoms to strengthen the Khalsa and further the cause of justice. He also initiated several social and religious reforms, such as the abolition of caste system and the establishment of equal rights for women.

Guru Gobind Singh's life was marked by several tragedies, including the martyrdom of his father, mother, and four sons. Despite these tragedies, he remained steadfast in his faith and his commitment to justice. His death, in 1708, was also a result of an assassination attempt by a member of his own community. However, his legacy lived on, and he became an inspiration for millions of Sikhs around the world.

Guru Gobind Singh's life and teachings have left a profound impact on Sikh history and culture. He is remembered as a true leader who dedicated his life to the service of humanity and the fight against oppression. His teachings continue to inspire people around the world, and his legacy is celebrated with great reverence and devotion by Sikhs everywhere.

1.3 Legends of Baba Banda Singh Bahadur

Baba Banda Singh Bahadur is a legendary figure in Sikh history, and his story is one of courage, faith, and perseverance. Born as Lachman Das in a Rajput family, he was trained as a warrior and had a natural talent for leadership. He converted to Sikhism after meeting Guru Gobind Singh and became one of his most trusted disciples.

After the brutal execution of Guru Gobind Singh's two younger sons, Baba Banda Singh Bahadur was entrusted with a mission to avenge their deaths and establish a just rule in the region. He was given the title of "Bahadur," meaning brave, by the Guru, and was told to lead a group of Sikhs to fight against the Mughal Empire, which had oppressed the local population.

Baba Banda Singh Bahadur and his followers launched a series of attacks against the Mughal army, which was then the most powerful military force in India. They fought with a ferocity and determination that surprised the enemy and inspired the local people to join their cause. Baba Banda Singh Bahadur was a charismatic leader who led from the front, and his army soon became a force to be reckoned with.

After several years of fighting, Baba Banda Singh Bahadur and his army finally defeated the Mughals in the battle of Chappar Chiri in 1710. He established the first Sikh state in Punjab, which was based on principles of equality, justice, and religious tolerance. He abolished the zamindari system, which had exploited the farmers, and replaced it with a system of communal land ownership. He also abolished the practice of untouchability and welcomed people of all castes and religions into his fold.

However, Baba Banda Singh Bahadur's success was short-lived. The Mughals launched a counter-attack, and after a long and brutal siege, his fortress was breached. Baba Banda Singh Bahadur was captured, and he and his followers were brutally executed by the Mughal emperor. But his legacy lived on, and he became an inspiration for future generations of Sikh warriors who would continue to fight for justice and freedom.

Baba Banda Singh Bahadur's life and legacy are a testament to the power of faith, courage, and determination. He proved that even the most powerful empire could be defeated by a small but determined group of people who were motivated by a just cause. His memory is still revered by millions of Sikhs around the world, and his story continues to inspire people to stand up against oppression and injustice.

1.4 Legendary Warrior Baba Deep Singh

Baba Deep Singh was a legendary Sikh warrior who is widely regarded as a symbol of courage, valor, and sacrifice. In contrast to other warriors, Baba Deep Singh stood out for his unwavering commitment to his faith and his community.

Unlike some warriors who fought for personal gain or power, Baba Deep Singh fought for a cause that was much larger than himself. He was a devout follower of Sikhism, and his life was guided by the principles of love, compassion, and service. He fought to defend his community and to uphold the values of justice and righteousness that he held dear.

Baba Deep Singh was also known for his remarkable sense of discipline and self-control. He was a skilled fighter, but he never used his skills for personal gain or revenge. Instead, he used them to protect his people and to uphold the principles of Sikhism. He was a leader who inspired others with his wisdom, his courage, and his unwavering devotion to his cause.

Baba Deep Singh was a Sikh warrior known for his courage, devotion, and sacrifice. In contrast to many other warriors, Baba Deep Singh fought not for personal gain or power, but for the ideals of Sikhism.

While some warriors may be driven by a desire for conquest or revenge, Baba Deep Singh fought for the defense of his religion and the protection of the Sikh way of life. He was a man of faith who believed in the importance of upholding the principles of Sikhism, even in the face of great adversity.

Unlike many warriors who may be motivated by individual glory or recognition, Baba Deep Singh was committed to the collective cause of his community. He saw himself as part of something larger than himself, and was willing to make great sacrifices for the betterment of the Sikh people.

Ultimately, Baba Deep Singh's legacy is not one of violence or conquest, but of selfless service and devotion to his faith. He serves as an inspiration to those who seek to uphold their ideals and beliefs, even in the face of great opposition.

Baba Deep Singh was a revered Sikh warrior who lived during the 18th century. In contrast to other warriors of his time, Baba Deep Singh was known for his spiritual strength and devotion to the Sikh religion.

While many warriors of his time were motivated by personal gain or glory, Baba Deep Singh fought for a higher cause. He was committed to defending the Sikh community and protecting their religious freedoms, even at the cost of his own life.

Baba Deep Singh also stood out from other warriors in his use of the sword. While many warriors of his time used the sword as a tool of violence and destruction, Baba Deep Singh saw the sword as a symbol of justice and protection. He believed that the sword should only be used in defense of the oppressed and never for personal gain.

Furthermore, Baba Deep Singh's commitment to his religion was an integral part of his identity as a warrior. He saw himself not just as a protector of his community, but also as a defender of the Sikh faith. He believed that his actions on the battlefield were a reflection of his devotion to God and his commitment to living a righteous life.

Baba Deep Singh was a revered Sikh warrior known for his valor and leadership in battles. In contrast to many other warriors, however, he was also a deeply spiritual and religious figure. While many warriors may have fought for personal gain or glory, Baba Deep Singh fought to defend the Sikh faith and its values. He was also known for his commitment to education and is credited with founding a number of schools and educational institutions. Overall, Baba Deep Singh represents a unique combination of martial prowess, religious devotion, and commitment to education and social justice.

Chapter Two : The Sikh Empire

Maharaja Ranjit Singh was the founder of the Sikh Empire in Punjab, which was one of the last great Indian empires before the British took control of the region. His reign marked a significant period of peace and prosperity in the region, and he is widely regarded as one of the greatest military leaders and statesmen in Indian history.

2.1 Early Life:

Ranjit Singh was born on November 13, 1780, in Gujranwala, a city in what is now Pakistan. He was born into a Punjabi Sikh family and was the only son of Sardar Maha Singh and Sardarni Mai Raj Kaur. His father was a small-time chieftain and had limited power and resources. Ranjit Singh inherited his father's territories at the age of 12, but he was still a young boy and had to rely on his mother and various advisers to govern his lands.

Family Background: Ranjit Singh was born into a Sikh family with a rich history of military and political leadership. His father, Maha Singh, was the founder of the Sukerchakia Misl, one of the twelve Sikh Misls (confederacies) that ruled over parts of the Punjab region.

Childhood and Education:

Ranjit Singh's mother died when he was only a year old, and he was brought up by his father and his grandmother. His father started training him in warfare and horsemanship at a young age, and he received further education from Sikh scholars.

Early Battles: Ranjit Singh's first military experience came at the age of 10 when he accompanied his father to battle against the Afghan chief, Zaman Khan. He also participated in battles against the Bhangi Misl, a rival Sikh confederacy.

Treaty with the British: In 1806, Ranjit Singh signed a treaty with the British East India Company, which recognized his authority over the Punjab region in exchange for his cooperation in maintaining British interests in the area

2.2 Rise to Power:

At the age of 16, Ranjit Singh captured Lahore, which was then ruled by the Afghans. This was a significant turning point in his life as it gave him control over the capital city of Punjab. He then spent the next several years consolidating his power and expanding his territories. He defeated the Mughals, the Afghans, and several other local chiefs, and by the time he was 21, he had established himself as the ruler of the entire Punjab region.

Expansion of the Sikh Empire:

Maharaja Ranjit Singh, the founder of the Sikh Empire, is widely known for expanding the Sikh Empire and unifying the various Sikh kingdoms in the Indian subcontinent.

With his power firmly established, Ranjit Singh began to expand his empire beyond the Punjab region. He conquered Kashmir in 1819 and brought it under his control. He also annexed several small states in the Himalayan region, including Kangra and Kullu. In 1831, he sent an expedition to Peshawar, which was then part of Afghanistan, and captured the city.Here is a detailed look at the expansion of the Sikh Empire under his leadership:

Consolidation of the Punjab:

Maharaja Ranjit Singh began his expansion by consolidating the various Sikh kingdoms in the Punjab region. He defeated the other Sikh rulers and brought them under his control, creating a unified Sikh state.

Conquest of Kashmir:

In 1819, Ranjit Singh's forces conquered the kingdom of Kashmir, which was a significant expansion of the Sikh Empire's territory. Kashmir remained a part of the Sikh Empire until the British took control of it in 1846.

Expansion into Afghanistan:

Maharaja Ranjit Singh also expanded the Sikh Empire into Afghanistan, conquering the city of Peshawar in 1834. This gave the Sikh Empire access to the trade routes that passed through Afghanistan, and helped to boost its economy.

Annexation of Multan and Sindh:

In 1818, Ranjit Singh's forces annexed the city of Multan, and in 1843, they conquered the province of Sindh. These conquests expanded the Sikh Empire's territory into modern-day Pakistan.

Control of the Northwest Frontier:

The Sikh Empire also gained control of the Northwest Frontier, which was a strategically important region. The Sikhs defeated the Afghan tribes in several battles, and brought the region under their control.

Trade and Diplomacy:

Maharaja Ranjit Singh also used trade and diplomacy to expand the Sikh Empire's influence. He established trade relationships with neighboring states, and negotiated treaties and alliances with them. This helped to establish the Sikh Empire as a major regional power.

Military Reforms:

Ranjit Singh was a great military leader, and he introduced several military reforms that helped him conquer new territories and establish a strong, centralized state. He organized his army along European lines and hired European officers to train his soldiers. He also introduced modern weapons, such as cannons and muskets, and established a disciplined, professional army that was loyal to him. Here is a detailed look at his military reforms:

Modernization of the Army:

Maharaja Ranjit Singh modernized the Sikh army by introducing European-style military training and tactics. He employed European officers, such as Jean-Francois Allard and Jean-Baptiste Ventura, to train his troops in modern military tactics.

Introduction of Cannons:

Under Ranjit Singh's leadership, the Sikh army was equipped with artillery, including cannons and mortars. These weapons were used to great effect in battles and sieges, and gave the Sikhs a significant advantage over their opponents.

Expansion of the Army:

Maharaja Ranjit Singh expanded the size of the Sikh army, recruiting soldiers from all walks of life, regardless of their caste or religion. This made the army more diverse and inclusive, and helped to build a sense of national identity and pride.

Reorganization of the Army:

Ranjit Singh reorganized the Sikh army into several divisions, each with its own command structure and set of responsibilities. This helped to streamline the army's operations and improve its efficiency.

Building of Forts:

Ranjit Singh built a series of forts and defensive structures along the borders of his empire, to protect it from outside threats. These forts were equipped with modern weaponry and were manned by well-trained soldiers.

Establishment of a Navy:

Ranjit Singh established a navy, which was used to patrol the rivers and canals of the Punjab region, and to protect his empire's trade routes. The navy was equipped with modern boats and weaponry, and was manned by well-trained sailors

Remarkable Battles:

Maharaja Ranjit Singh, the founder of the Sikh Empire, fought numerous battles throughout his reign to expand his territory and consolidate his power. Here's a detailed storyline of some of the significant battles fought by him:

Battle of Sujanpur (1809): In 1809, Ranjit Singh's army under the command of General Amar Singh attacked the fort of Sujanpur, which was held by the Raja of Kangra. The fort was well-fortified and heavily defended, but after a six-month siege, Ranjit Singh's army was able to breach the defenses and capture the fort.

Battle of Multan (1818): In 1818, Ranjit Singh launched an attack on the city of Multan, which was ruled by the Afghan ruler, Muzaffar Khan. After a prolonged siege, Ranjit Singh's forces were able to breach the walls and capture the city. This battle marked the beginning of Ranjit Singh's control over the entire Punjab region.

Battle of Attock (1813): The Battle of Attock was fought between Ranjit Singh and the Afghan ruler, Dost Muhammad Khan. The Afghans had a much larger force, but Ranjit Singh's army was able to hold them off long enough for the river to rise and cut off their retreat, forcing them to surrender.

Battle of Naushera (1823): The Battle of Naushera was fought between Ranjit Singh and the Afghan ruler, Yar Muhammad Khan. Ranjit Singh's army was able to defeat the Afghan forces and capture the city of Naushera, which gave him control over the strategic Khyber Pass.

Battle of Peshawar (1834): The Battle of Peshawar was fought between Ranjit Singh and the Durrani Empire. Ranjit Singh's army was able to defeat the Durrani forces and capture the city of Peshawar, which gave him control over the entire Khyber region.

Battle of Jamrud (1837): The Battle of Jamrud was fought between Ranjit Singh's army and the Durrani Empire. The Sikhs were able to defeat the Durrani forces, but Ranjit Singh himself was injured in the battle and later died in 1839.

2.3 Religious Tolerance:

Ranjit Singh was a devout Sikh, but he was also known for his religious tolerance. He appointed Muslims and Hindus to high positions in his government and military, and he treated all religions equally. He also funded the construction of several religious buildings, including the Golden Temple in Amritsar, which is considered the holiest site in Sikhism.

Maharaja Ranjit Singh, the founder of the Sikh Empire, is widely known for his religious tolerance and his patronage of all religions. He believed that all religions were equal and deserved respect and support. Here is an in-depth look at his religious tolerance:

Support for Other Religions: Ranjit Singh was a staunch follower of Sikhism, but he also supported other religions. He donated funds for the construction of temples, mosques, and gurdwaras, and his court was open to scholars and intellectuals of all faiths.

The Lahore Darbar: Ranjit Singh's court, known as the Lahore Darbar, was known for its religious diversity. It was home to scholars, poets, and artists from all religions, and it was a center of learning and culture.

Sikhism and Hinduism: Ranjit Singh believed that Sikhism and Hinduism were closely related, and he encouraged the integration of the two religions. He allowed Hindu priests to perform religious rituals in Sikh temples, and he himself participated in Hindu festivals and rituals.

Relations with Muslims: Despite the history of conflict between the Sikhs and the Muslims, Ranjit Singh was known for his friendly relations with Muslims. He appointed Muslims to high positions in his court and military, and he built mosques and other Islamic structures.

The Golden Temple: The Golden Temple in Amritsar, the most sacred site in Sikhism, was renovated and expanded under Ranjit Singh's patronage. He donated funds for the construction of the temple, and he made sure that it was accessible to all Sikhs, regardless of their caste or social status.

Support for Education: Ranjit Singh was a strong advocate of education, and he encouraged the establishment of schools and colleges for all religions. He donated funds for the construction of schools and libraries, and he made sure that education was accessible to all.

In conclusion, Maharaja Ranjit Singh's religious tolerance was a key aspect of his reign. He believed that all religions were equal and deserving of respect, and he supported the construction of religious structures for all faiths. His legacy as a tolerant and enlightened leader continues to inspire many to this day

2.4 Death:

Maharaja Ranjit Singh was the founder of the Sikh Empire in India and ruled from 1801 until his death in 1839. His death was a significant event in the history of India as it led to the decline of the Sikh Empire and a period of instability in the region.

Ranjit Singh's health had been declining for several years before his death. He suffered from a variety of ailments, including a loss of eyesight in one eye, gout, and liver problems. Despite his health problems, he continued to be an active ruler and participated in the administration of the empire.

In the summer of 1838, Ranjit Singh's health took a turn for the worse. He was suffering from severe liver problems and was bedridden for several weeks. His condition worsened, and his physicians were unable to provide any relief. In June 1839, Ranjit Singh's condition deteriorated further, and he became unconscious.

His son, Kharak Singh, took over the administration of the empire while his father was ill. Kharak Singh was not a capable ruler, and his reign was marked by corruption and incompetence. He was heavily influenced by his advisor, Raja Dhian Singh, who was unpopular with the people.

On June 27, 1839, Ranjit Singh died at the age of 59. His death was a significant loss for the Sikh Empire, as he was a strong and capable ruler who had maintained stability in the region for many years. With his death, the Sikh Empire began to decline, and the British began to exert more influence in the region.

Ranjit Singh was cremated in Lahore, and his ashes were scattered in the Sutlej River. His death was mourned by people across India, including Hindus and Muslims, who respected him as a just and fair ruler. Today, he is remembered as a significant figure in the history of India, and his legacy continues to inspire people around the world.

Chapter Three : The Khalsa

The Khalsa is a military force established by Guru Gobind Singh in 1699 in what is now the Punjab region of India and Pakistan. This force was created to defend the Sikh community against external threats and to promote the principles of equality, justice, and righteousness. The establishment of the Khalsa was a significant event in Sikh history, and it continues to be an important symbol of Sikh identity and strength.

At the heart of the Khalsa is the concept of the Panj Pyare, or the "Five Beloved Ones." These were five Sikhs who were chosen by Guru Gobind Singh to initiate the Khalsa by undergoing a special ceremony known as Amrit Sanchar. During this ceremony, the Panj Pyare prepared a special mixture of sugar and water known as Amrit, which they stirred with a double-edged sword while reciting prayers from the Sikh holy book, the Guru Granth Sahib. They then drank from the Amrit and were given new names that included the suffix "Singh," which means "lion."

The Khalsa was a unique force in many ways. It was open to people of all castes and backgrounds, and it was founded on the principles of equality and justice. Members of the Khalsa were expected to follow a strict code of conduct that included abstaining from alcohol and drugs, refraining from adultery, and maintaining a high level of personal hygiene. They were also expected to wear the five Ks, which included Kesh (uncut hair), Kanga (a wooden comb), Kara (a steel bracelet), Kachera (a special type of underwear), and Kirpan (a ceremonial sword).

One of the most significant roles of the Khalsa was to defend the Sikh community against external threats. This was particularly important in a time of political instability and religious conflict. The Khalsa fought in a number of battles, including the battles of Bhangani, Nadaun, and Chamkaur. In these battles, the Khalsa demonstrated its bravery, discipline, and military prowess.

In conclusion, the Khalsa is an important symbol of Sikh identity and strength. It was founded on the principles of equality, justice, and righteousness, and it played a vital role in defending the Sikh community against external threats. The Khalsa is an inspiration to Sikhs around the world, and it continues to be a source of pride and strength for the Sikh community. If you are a Sikh, I urge you to learn more about the Khalsa and the important role it played in Sikh history. If you are not a Sikh, I encourage you to learn more about this fascinating and unique military force and the values that it represents.

3.1 The Story Begins:

The story of the Khalsa and how Guru Gobind Singh ji transformed them into warriors is a fascinating and inspiring one.

In the late 17th century, the Mughal Empire ruled over much of India, and the Sikh community was facing persecution and oppression. The Sikhs were often subjected to violence and discrimination, and their religious practices were banned.

In 1699, Guru Gobind Singh ji called together a large gathering of Sikhs in the town of Anandpur Sahib. The Guru knew that the Sikh community needed to be strong and united to resist the oppression they were facing, and he had a plan to create a new type of warrior that would be able to defend the community and uphold the principles of righteousness and justice.

At the gathering, Guru Gobind Singh ji presented himself before the assembled Sikhs and asked for a volunteer who was prepared to give his life for the Guru. One man, called Daya Ram, came forward and offered his head to the Guru. Guru Gobind Singh ji took Daya Ram into a tent and emerged shortly afterwards with a bloody sword. He repeated his request two more times, and two more men came forward, each of whom the Guru took into the tent and emerged with a bloody sword.

The Guru then revealed the three men, who were unharmed, and they were now dressed in blue garments, turbans, and a special bangle. The Guru called them the Panj Pyare or the Five Beloved Ones. The Guru then asked the Panj Pyare to initiate him into the new order and to baptize him with Amrit or nectar. The Panj Pyare prepared the Amrit in a vessel and stirred it with a double-edged sword while reciting hymns from the Sikh scripture. The Guru drank from the vessel and then asked the Panj Pyare to be initiated into the Khalsa in the same manner.

After this, the Guru gave the Khalsa a new code of conduct, which included following the principles of truth, justice, and righteousness. The Khalsa were to wear five symbols of their faith, known as the five Ks, which included uncut hair, a comb, a steel bracelet, a special type of undergarment, and a ceremonial sword. The Guru declared that all members of the Khalsa were to be considered equals, regardless of their caste, background, or gender.

With this new order of warriors, the Guru transformed the Sikh community into a powerful and unified force. The Khalsa were trained in the arts of war and became a formidable army that was able to resist the oppression of the Mughals and other oppressors. They fought bravely in numerous battles, defending their faith and their people.

In conclusion, the story of the Khalsa and how Guru Gobind Singh ji created them as warriors is a powerful testament to the strength of faith and the courage of those who are willing to stand up against oppression and injustice. The Khalsa continue to be an inspiration to Sikhs around the world, and their legacy lives on in the values of equality, justice, and righteousness that they uphold.

3.2 The Battle Against Truth

After Guru Gobind Singh ji established the Khalsa, the Sikh community underwent a remarkable transformation. The Khalsa were no longer a group of passive followers, but instead they became active participants in the struggle for freedom and justice. They fought courageously against their oppressors and inspired others to do the same.

Under the leadership of the Khalsa, the Sikhs became a force to be reckoned with. They fought numerous battles against the Mughals and other oppressors, and despite being outnumbered and outgunned, they emerged victorious time and time again. The Khalsa's courage and determination became legendary, and their successes inspired others to join their cause.

The Khalsa were not just warriors, however. They were also deeply committed to their faith and to the principles of equality and justice. They worked tirelessly to promote these values, both within the Sikh community and beyond. They established schools and other educational institutions, and they promoted the development of arts and culture.

The Khalsa also played a significant role in the political and social life of India. They established a form of self-government known as the Misls, which allowed them to rule their own territories and defend themselves against outside threats. The Misls also worked together to promote the welfare of the Sikh community and to advance the cause of freedom and justice.

Over time, the Khalsa evolved and adapted to changing circumstances. They continued to fight for their rights and freedoms, even as they faced new challenges and threats. They became known for their bravery and their unwavering commitment to their principles, and their legacy lives on to this day.

The first major battle fought by the Khalsa warriors was the Battle of Bhangani in 1688. It was a significant event in the history of the Sikh faith and marked the beginning of a new era in the struggle for freedom and justice.

The battle was sparked by the actions of Wazir Khan, the Mughal governor of Sirhind. Wazir Khan was a staunch opponent of Guru Gobind Singh, the leader of the Sikh community, and he had ordered his soldiers to attack the Sikhs and their supporters in the town of Anandpur Sahib.

Guru Gobind Singh, who had been preparing his followers for the struggle ahead, decided that it was time to take a stand against the oppression. He gathered his followers, who had taken an oath of allegiance to him and his cause, and led them into battle against the Mughal army.

The Khalsa warriors were outnumbered and outgunned, but they fought with a fierce determination and a courage born of faith. They charged the Mughal army with swords drawn, and soon the air was filled with the clash of steel and the cries of the wounded.

The battle raged for several hours, but in the end, the Khalsa emerged victorious. They had driven the Mughal army back and had inflicted heavy losses on their enemies.

The Battle of Bhangani was a significant victory for the Khalsa warriors. It demonstrated their courage and determination in the face of overwhelming odds, and it marked the beginning of a new era in the struggle for freedom and justice. It was a turning point in the history of the Sikh faith, and it inspired many more Sikhs to join the cause and fight for their rights and freedoms.

The legacy of the Khalsa warriors continues to inspire and empower Sikhs around the world to this day. The lessons of courage, determination, and faith that they embodied are an enduring legacy that has stood the test of time.

The Khalsa warriors, led by Guru Gobind Singh ji, fought many battles against the Mughal and other oppressive forces in the late 17th and early 18th centuries. After the Battle of Bhangani, the Khalsa continued to grow in strength and numbers, and their bravery and determination inspired more and more people to join their cause.

The second major battle fought by the Khalsa was the Battle of Nadaun in 1691. In this battle, the Khalsa faced a combined Mughal and Hill Rajput army, which greatly outnumbered them. Despite being heavily outnumbered, the Khalsa fought bravely and fiercely and were able to repel the enemy, showing their military prowess.

However, the Khalsa faced many challenges in the following years, including a siege of their stronghold at Anandpur Sahib in 1700. The Khalsa warriors held out for several months against the Mughal army, but they were eventually forced to retreat due to a lack of supplies. This was a major setback for the Khalsa, but it did not diminish their determination to fight for their rights and freedoms.

In 1704, one of the most famous battles fought by the Khalsa took place at Chamkaur. Guru Gobind

Singh ji and a small group of Khalsa warriors were trapped in a fortress by a much larger Mughal army. The Khalsa fought bravely, and many of them gave their lives in the battle. Guru Gobind Singh ji also lost his two elder sons in this battle, but he refused to be defeated and continued to inspire his followers to fight on.

The Khalsa warriors continued to face many challenges in the years that followed, including the martyrdom of Guru Tegh Bahadur, the ninth Sikh guru, and the execution of Banda Singh Bahadur, a prominent Khalsa warrior. Despite these setbacks, the Khalsa continued to grow in strength and numbers, and their bravery and determination inspired many more Sikhs to join their cause.

In the end, the Khalsa warriors were able to overcome the forces of oppression and establish a free and independent Sikh state in Punjab. Their legacy of bravery and determination lives on to this day, inspiring

Sikhs around the world to fight for their rights and freedoms. The story of the Khalsa warriors is one of courage, determination, and faith, and it will continue to inspire future generations of Sikhs for years to come.

In conclusion, the story of the Khalsa after it was established by Guru Gobind Singh ji is a fascinating and inspiring one. The Khalsa's courage, determination, and commitment to their principles transformed the Sikh community and helped to shape the course of Indian history. Their legacy lives on in the values of equality, justice, and freedom that they fought so hard to uphold.

3.3 Story Continued : Battle of Khalsa warriors

After the passing of Guru Gobind Singh ji in 1708, the Khalsa warriors continued to fight for their rights and freedoms. They faced many challenges in the years that followed, including the invasion of Punjab by Afghan forces in the early 18th century. The Khalsa warriors fought bravely against these invaders, and they were eventually able to drive them out of the region.

One of the most famous battles fought by the Khalsa warriors in this period was the Battle of Muktsar in 1705. In this battle, a group of Khalsa warriors led by Baba Deep Singh fought against a Mughal army, and they were able to achieve a decisive victory. Baba Deep Singh is remembered as one of the most revered Khalsa warriors, and his bravery and sacrifice continue to inspire Sikhs to this day.

In the years that followed, the Khalsa warriors also faced internal divisions and conflicts. However, they remained committed to their cause, and they were able to establish a free and independent Sikh state in Punjab in the late 18th century. This state was known as the Sikh Empire, and it was ruled by Maharaja Ranjit Singh, a prominent Khalsa leader.

Under the leadership of Maharaja Ranjit Singh, the Khalsa warriors were able to achieve many great accomplishments. They expanded their territory, built a strong and prosperous empire, and defended their rights and freedoms against foreign invaders. They also made significant contributions to the arts, culture, and architecture of Punjab, leaving behind a rich legacy that continues to inspire Sikhs around the world.

One of the most famous achievements of the Khalsa warriors under Maharaja Ranjit Singh was the construction of the Golden Temple in Amritsar. This temple, which is considered one of the holiest places of worship for Sikhs, was built with the contributions of many Khalsa leaders and warriors.

The Khalsa warriors also made significant contributions to the military history of India. They developed a unique form of warfare known as the Khalsa style of fighting, which emphasized courage, bravery, and discipline. This style of fighting was instrumental in the Khalsa warriors' many victories against their enemies.

In conclusion, the Khalsa warriors played a significant role in the history of India and the Sikh faith. They fought bravely and fiercely for their rights and freedoms, and they achieved many great accomplishments in the face of overwhelming odds. Their legacy of courage, determination, and faith continues to inspire Sikhs around the world to this day.

3.4 The End Of Sikh Empire

The decline of the Sikh leadership after the death of Maharaja Ranjit Singh in 1839. His successors were unable to maintain the unity and strength of the empire, and they faced increasing challenges from British colonial forces in India.

The Khalsa Empire was a shining example of the strength and resilience of the Sikh people. After many years of struggle and sacrifice, they had established a free and independent state in Punjab, and they were ruled by the wise and just Maharaja Ranjit Singh.

Under the leadership of Maharaja Ranjit Singh, the Khalsa Empire flourished. They built a strong and prosperous economy, and they made significant contributions to the arts, culture, and architecture of Punjab. They were also renowned for their military strength, and they were able to defend their territory against foreign invaders.

However, the end of the Khalsa Empire came swiftly and unexpectedly. After the passing of Maharaja Ranjit Singh in 1839, the empire was left without a strong and capable leader. This created a power vacuum that was quickly filled by British colonial forces.

The British were determined to annex the Khalsa Empire, and they began a series of wars and conflicts that eventually led to the downfall of the Sikh state. The First Anglo-Sikh War was fought in 1845, and although the Khalsa forces put up a valiant fight, they were ultimately defeated. The Treaty of Lahore was signed, which forced the Sikhs to cede significant portions of their territory to the British.

The British saw the Sikh Empire as a threat to their own interests in India, and they began a campaign of military conquest in the region. The two sides clashed in a number of battles, including the First AngloSikh War in 1845-46, which saw the British emerge victorious. The Sikhs were forced to cede control of parts of their territory to the British, and they were required to pay a heavy indemnity to cover the costs of the war.

The Sikhs, however, were not ones to give up easily. They continued to resist British rule, and the Second Anglo-Sikh War was fought in 1848. Once again, the Khalsa warriors fought with bravery and determination, but they were ultimately defeated by the superior firepower and tactics of the British forces.

The Sikhs continued to resist British rule, and they fought in the Second Anglo-Sikh War in 1848-49. This conflict saw the Sikhs suffer a major defeat, and they were forced to surrender control of their remaining territory to the British. The Sikh Empire officially came to an end in 1849, when the British annexed Punjab and incorporated it into British India.

In the aftermath of the Second Anglo-Sikh War, the Khalsa Empire was dissolved, and Punjab was annexed by the British. This was a dark chapter in the history of the Sikh people, but they continued to resist and fight for their rights and freedoms.

The legacy of the Khalsa Empire lives on, and the bravery and sacrifice of the Khalsa warriors continue to inspire Sikhs around the world. Despite the challenges and hardships they faced, the Sikhs never gave up, and they continue to fight for justice and equality to this day.

The end of the Khalsa Empire was a significant blow to the Sikh community, and it marked a major turning point in the history of the region. The Sikhs faced a period of political, social, and economic upheaval in the years that followed, as they struggled to come to terms with the loss of their independence and the challenges of living under British rule.

However, the legacy of the Khalsa Empire and the Khalsa warriors continued to inspire the Sikh community, and it played an important role in the struggle for Indian independence in the 20th century. The ideals of courage, bravery, and self-determination that were embodied by the Khalsa warriors remain a central part of the Sikh faith and continue to guide and inspire the Sikh community today.

Chapter Four : The Rebellion of 1857

The Rebellion of 1857, also known as the Indian Mutiny or the First War of Indian Independence, was a significant event in the history of India. It began as a mutiny among the Indian soldiers in the British East India Company's army, but quickly spread to involve civilians, including peasants, landowners, and princes. The rebellion lasted for over a year and resulted in widespread violence and bloodshed, with both sides committing atrocities. The causes of the rebellion were complex and varied, but they were rooted in the economic, social, and cultural changes that were taking place in India at the time. The British had been in India for over 200 years by the mid-19th century, and their policies of economic exploitation, cultural imperialism, and religious intolerance had created deep resentment among the Indian people.

The rebellion was a turning point in the history of India. It led to the end of the East India Company's rule and the beginning of direct British rule over India. It also spurred the growth of Indian nationalism and the rise of figures such as Mahatma Gandhi, who would lead India to independence nearly a century later.

The origins of the Rebellion of 1857 can be traced back to a number of factors, including political, economic, social, and cultural changes in India during the early to mid-19th century. The events leading up to the outbreak of the rebellion were complex and multifaceted, but some key moments and factors can be identified.

One major factor was the policy of annexation pursued by the British East India Company. In the years leading up to the rebellion, the Company had annexed a number of Indian states, often using questionable methods, which created resentment among Indian rulers and their subjects. The annexation of the state of Oudh in 1856, which deprived the ruler of his throne and led to the disbanding of his army, was a particularly significant event that helped spark the rebellion.

Another important factor was the introduction of the new Enfield rifle by the British, which used a cartridge greased with animal fat. The use of animal fat, which was prohibited in both Hindu and Muslim religions, led to concerns among Indian soldiers that the British were trying to convert them to Christianity. This sparked a mutiny among the soldiers in the town of Meerut on May 10, 1857, which quickly spread to other parts of northern and central India.

The rebellion was not just a military mutiny, however. It was also fueled by social and economic grievances, including the displacement of Indian artisans and the exploitation of Indian peasants by British landlords and moneylenders. In many areas, local elites and leaders, such as the Rani of Jhansi, joined the rebellion and provided important leadership.

Overall, the events leading up to the Rebellion of 1857 were shaped by a range of factors, including political and economic grievances, religious and cultural tensions, and local and regional dynamics. The mutiny of Indian soldiers in Meerut on May 10, 1857, marked the beginning of a broader rebellion that would have far-reaching consequences for India and the British Empire.

4.1 The Punjabi Faces Of 1857 Rebellion

The Rebellion of 1857, also known as the Indian Mutiny or the First War of Indian Independence, involved a diverse range of actors from different regions and communities of India. Among those who played a significant role in the rebellion were several Punjabi leaders and soldiers who came from the region of Punjab, which was then part of the Sikh Empire.

The Punjabi faces of the rebellion include notable figures such as Rani Jindan Kaur, the widow of Maharaja Ranjit Singh who provided financial and material support to the rebels and encouraged Punjabi soldiers to join the uprising. Another significant Punjabi leader was Diwan Mul Raj, who was the governor of the Jalandhar Doab region and led an uprising in his region. Mangal Pandey, a famous sepoy, was also part of a unit that included many Punjabi soldiers who participated in the mutiny.

These and other Punjabi figures played important roles in shaping the course of the uprising in northern India, showing the significance of Punjabi resistance and rebellion in Indian history. Their contributions remain an important symbol of resistance and rebellion, and their stories continue to inspire and influence Punjabi and Indian culture today.

4.1.1 Rani Jindan Kaur

Rani Jindan Kaur was a significant political figure and a symbol of resistance during the Rebellion of 1857 in northern India. She was the widow of Maharaja Ranjit Singh, the founder of the Sikh Empire, and had been exiled to Nepal after his death in 1839. However, she returned to Lahore in 1846 and became involved in politics, particularly in support of her son, Maharaja Duleep Singh, who had been installed on the throne at the age of five.

During the Rebellion of 1857, Rani Jindan Kaur played a key role in supporting the uprising against the British. She used her personal wealth and resources to provide financial and material support to the rebels, including weapons, horses, and other supplies. She also encouraged Punjabi soldiers to join the uprising and provided leadership and guidance to the rebels.

One of her most significant contributions to the rebellion was her role in the siege of Delhi, which had been taken over by rebel forces in May 1857. Rani Jindan Kaur arrived in Delhi in August of that year and immediately began organizing support for the rebels. She used her personal connections and resources to provide food, shelter, and medical care for the rebels, many of whom were wounded or sick.

She also encouraged the Sikh soldiers who had joined the British forces to switch sides and support the rebels. This was a significant achievement, given the tensions between the Sikh community and the rebels, many of whom were Muslim. Her efforts helped to unite different communities and regions in the rebellion and played a crucial role in the capture of Delhi by the rebels in September 1857.

After the fall of Delhi, Rani Jindan Kaur continued to support the rebels and provided financial and material assistance to various groups throughout northern India. However, her role in the rebellion also brought her into conflict with other leaders, particularly the male leaders of the Sikh community, who viewed her as a threat to their own power.

In 1858, Rani Jindan Kaur was captured by the British and sent to exile in England. She lived there for the rest of her life and died in 1863. Despite her exile, she remains a symbol of resistance and rebellion in Indian history and is often remembered as a key figure in the Rebellion of 1857. Her contributions to the uprising helped to unite different communities and regions and showed the potential for political and social change in India.

4.1.2 Diwan Mul Raj

Diwan Mul Raj was a prominent leader during the Rebellion of 1857 in northern India, who played a significant role in organizing and supporting the uprising against British colonial rule. He was born in the city of Jammu, in present-day Jammu and Kashmir, and began his career in the court of Raja Gulab Singh, who had established the princely state of Jammu and Kashmir.

During the 1857 rebellion, Diwan Mul Raj played a key role in organizing and mobilizing rebel forces in the Jammu region, where he enjoyed considerable influence and support. He used his position as the chief minister of Jammu and Kashmir to encourage the local population to rise up against the British and to provide leadership and guidance to the rebels.

Under his leadership, the rebels in the Jammu region were able to capture several strategic locations, including the city of Sialkot, which was a key British military base. Diwan Mul Raj also organized and led several successful guerrilla attacks against British troops, which helped to disrupt their supply lines and communication networks.

One of his most significant contributions to the rebellion was his role in the Battle of Sialkot, which took place in July 1857. The battle was fought between the rebel forces under Diwan Mul Raj and a British force led by Brigadier-General John Nicholson. Despite being outnumbered and outgunned, the rebels were able to inflict heavy losses on the British and forced them to retreat.

However, the rebellion in the Jammu region was eventually suppressed by the British, who captured Diwan Mul Raj and executed him in 1858. His execution was seen as a significant blow to the rebellion and a sign of British victory. Nevertheless, his contributions to the uprising helped to inspire others to join the rebellion and showed the potential for resistance and rebellion against British colonial rule.

Diwan Mul Raj remains a symbol of resistance and rebellion in Indian history, particularly in the Jammu and Kashmir region. His life and legacy serve as a reminder of the importance of political and social change and the need to resist oppression and injustice.

4.1.3 Mangal Pandey

Mangal Pandey was a key figure in the Rebellion of 1857, known for his role in sparking the uprising against British colonial rule in northern India. He was born in the village of Nagwa in present-day Uttar Pradesh, and joined the British East India Company's army as a sepoy in 1849.

Pandey played a significant role in the events that led up to the rebellion. In March 1857, he became disillusioned with the British and incited a mutiny among his fellow sepoys at the Barrackpore cantonment, near Calcutta. He defied his commanding officer and led a group of sepoys in refusing to use the newly-issued Enfield rifles, which were rumored to be greased with pig and cow fat, a religiously sensitive issue for both Hindu and Muslim sepoys.

The British authorities reacted swiftly to the mutiny, and Pandey was arrested and sentenced to death. However, his actions had already inspired other sepoys to join the rebellion, which soon spread to other parts of northern India.

Pandey's defiance and courage became a symbol of resistance and rebellion, and he is often regarded as the first martyr of the Indian Rebellion of 1857. His story inspired other Indian soldiers to join the rebellion, and he is remembered for his bravery and sacrifice in the fight against British colonial rule.

Despite the British efforts to suppress his legacy, Pandey's story has continued to inspire Indian nationalists and freedom fighters. He is remembered as a hero in Indian history, and his name has become synonymous with the struggle for Indian independence. The story of Mangal Pandey is a powerful reminder of the importance of resistance and the sacrifices made by those who fought for India's freedom.

4.1.4 Mian Meer

Mian Meer was a prominent Sufi saint and spiritual leader during the Rebellion of 1857 in northern India. He was born in Lahore in present-day Pakistan, and was known for his devotion to God and his teachings of tolerance and compassion.

During the rebellion, Mian Meer played an important role in providing moral and spiritual support to the rebels. He was a trusted advisor to many of the key rebel leaders, and his spiritual influence helped to inspire and motivate the rebels in their fight against British colonial rule.

Mian Meer was also involved in the organization of rebel forces in the Punjab region. He worked closely with leaders such as Rani Jindan Kaur and Diwan Mul Raj to mobilize and organize the rebel forces, and provided financial and material support to the cause.

Despite the risks to his safety and well-being, Mian Meer openly declared his support for the rebellion and refused to collaborate with the British authorities. He was eventually arrested by the British and sentenced to imprisonment in the Lahore Fort, where he spent several months before being released.

Mian Meer's contributions to the Rebellion of 1857 were significant, and his spiritual guidance and support helped to inspire and motivate the rebels in their fight for freedom. His legacy as a Sufi saint and spiritual leader continues to inspire people in the region and beyond, and his story serves as a reminder of the importance of faith and spirituality in the struggle against oppression and injustice.

4.1.5 Lal Singh

Lal Singh was one of the prominent Sikh leaders during the Rebellion of 1857 in northern India. He was born in Punjab and was known for his bravery, military skills, and leadership abilities.

During the rebellion, Lal Singh played a crucial role in organizing the Sikh forces to join the rebel cause. He was a trusted advisor to the key rebel leaders, including Rani Jindan Kaur and Diwan Mul Raj, and his military expertise helped to strengthen the rebel forces in the Punjab region.

Lal Singh was also instrumental in the capture of the strategic city of Delhi, which was a major victory for the rebel forces. He led a contingent of Sikh soldiers who played a key role in the battle, and his bravery and tactical skills helped to turn the tide of the conflict in favor of the rebels.

Despite the successes of the rebel forces in the early stages of the uprising, the British eventually regained control of the region and suppressed the rebellion. Lal Singh was captured and imprisoned, along with other rebel leaders, and he was eventually exiled to Rangoon in present-day Myanmar.

Lal Singh's contributions to the Rebellion of 1857 were significant, and his leadership and military skills helped to mobilize and organize the rebel forces in the Punjab region. His bravery and tactical abilities were key to the early successes of the rebellion, and his legacy as a Sikh leader and freedom fighter continues to inspire people in the region and beyond.

4.2 The Forces Of Mutiny

The Indian Rebellion of 1857, also known as the Indian Mutiny, was a significant uprising against British colonial rule in India. The rebellion involved a diverse range of forces, including soldiers, civilians, and rebel leaders who were united in their opposition to British imperial rule.

The rebellion was sparked by a range of factors, including economic exploitation, religious tensions, and a growing sense of Indian nationalism. The sepoys, or Indian soldiers, played a key role in the rebellion, with many of them joining the revolt and refusing to obey British orders. The sepoys were joined by other groups, including peasants, artisans, and landowners, who were also discontented with British rule.

The rebellion was marked by a series of battles and skirmishes, with rebel forces often outnumbered and outgunned by the British. However, the rebels were able to capture several key cities and strategic locations, including Delhi and Kanpur, which helped to bolster their cause and inspire other groups to join the uprising.

The rebel forces were led by a diverse range of leaders, including Rani Jindan Kaur, Diwan Mul Raj, and Nana Sahib, among others. These leaders were able to mobilize and organize the rebel forces, and their military skills and strategic thinking helped to keep the rebellion going for several months.

Despite their initial successes, the rebel forces were eventually defeated by the British, who were able to mobilize their vast military resources and crush the rebellion. Many of the rebel leaders were captured and executed, and the rebellion marked a turning point in the history of British colonial rule in India.

The forces of the mutiny were driven by a shared sense of frustration and discontent with British rule, and their rebellion was a powerful statement of Indian resistance to colonialism. The Indian Rebellion of 1857 remains a significant event in Indian history, and its legacy continues to inspire people in India and around the world to fight for freedom and justice.

4.2.1 Sepoys

Sepoys played a significant role in the Indian Rebellion of 1857. They were Indian soldiers who were employed by the British East India Company and were often used to maintain colonial control over the Indian population. The word "sepoy" comes from the Persian word "sipahi," which means soldier.

The sepoys were recruited from different regions of India and came from various backgrounds, including Hindu, Muslim, and Sikh communities. They were trained in the British military tradition and were often used to suppress local uprisings and rebellions.

However, the sepoys became increasingly disillusioned with British colonial rule and its policies. There were several reasons for their discontent, including low wages, poor living conditions, and lack of promotions. Furthermore, the sepoys were also unhappy with the attempts to impose British culture and religion on them, such as the use of animal fat in the cartridges of their rifles, which was offensive to both Hindu and Muslim soldiers.

In 1857, the discontent among the sepoys reached a boiling point, and they joined the Indian Rebellion against the British. The sepoys played a significant role in the early stages of the rebellion, as they were the most organized and disciplined force available to the rebels. They launched coordinated attacks on British military installations and officers and succeeded in capturing several key locations.

However, the sepoys were ultimately defeated by the better-equipped and more experienced British military. Many sepoys were captured and executed, while others fled to their homes and villages.

The sepoys' role in the Indian Rebellion of 1857 was complex, and their motivations varied. Some sepoys joined the rebellion out of a sense of patriotism and a desire to overthrow British colonial rule, while others were motivated by personal grievances and dissatisfaction with their working conditions. Nonetheless, the sepoys played a significant role in the rebellion and their contributions continue to be remembered in India as a symbol of resistance against British colonialism.

4.2.2 The Civilian Population

The civilian population played a significant role in the Indian Rebellion of 1857. They were composed of a diverse group of people, including peasants, artisans, and landowners, who were dissatisfied with British colonial rule and sought to overthrow it.

The British colonial rule in India had brought many changes, including land revenue policies, which forced many farmers to give up their land and become sharecroppers, and the introduction of new taxes, which increased the burden on the common people. The British colonial authorities also imposed their culture, language, and religion, which further alienated the local population. All of these factors contributed to the growing discontent among the civilian population, and they were ready to revolt against the British.

During the Indian Rebellion of 1857, the civilian population rose up against the British colonial authorities. They joined the rebels in large numbers and provided crucial support in the form of food, shelter, and other supplies. They also played a significant role in the attacks on British military installations and the killing of British officials.

The civilian population was particularly active in the rural areas, where the British had not yet established complete control. They formed guerrilla groups and attacked British supply lines, disrupted communications, and ambushed British patrols. These actions forced the British to divert their military resources, which weakened their grip on other areas.

The civilian population also played a crucial role in spreading the message of rebellion and inspiring others to join the cause. They used songs, folktales, and other forms of cultural expression to mobilize the masses and create a sense of unity among the diverse groups of people.

The civilian population's contribution to the Indian Rebellion of 1857 was significant, and their bravery and sacrifice continue to inspire people in India and around the world. Their participation in the rebellion marked the beginning of a new era in Indian history, one that saw the people of India standing up against colonial oppression and fighting for their rights and freedom.

4.2.3 The Rebel Leaders

The Indian Rebellion of 1857 had several rebel leaders who played a crucial role in organizing and leading the revolt against the British colonial authorities. These leaders came from different backgrounds, including the nobility, the military, and the civilian population. They united in their opposition to British colonial rule and inspired others to join the rebellion.

One of the most well-known rebel leaders was Rani Lakshmibai of Jhansi. She was the queen of the princely state of Jhansi and became one of the symbols of the Indian Rebellion. She led her troops into battle and fought bravely against the British forces. Her leadership and bravery inspired many others to join the rebellion.

Another important rebel leader was Nana Sahib, the adopted son of the last Peshwa, the ruler of the Maratha Empire. Nana Sahib's leadership was crucial in the early stages of the rebellion, as he coordinated attacks on British military installations and played a key role in the capture of Cawnpore.

However, he was later forced to flee to Nepal after the British regained control of the region.

Tantia Tope was another rebel leader who played a significant role in the Indian Rebellion. He was a close associate of Nana Sahib and became one of the key leaders after Sahib's departure. Tope led his forces in several successful battles against the British and was known for his tactical skills and military strategy.

Other notable rebel leaders included Kunwar Singh, who led a rebellion in Bihar; Maulvi Ahmedullah Shah, who led a rebellion in the Awadh region; and Bakht Khan, who led the rebel forces in Delhi.

These rebel leaders were instrumental in the Indian Rebellion of 1857. They inspired and mobilized the masses, organized military operations, and provided leadership in the face of adversity. Their contributions continue to be remembered in India as a symbol of resistance against colonialism and imperialism.

4.2.4 The Local Rulers

The local rulers played a significant role in the Indian Rebellion of 1857, as they were among the primary victims of British colonial policies. Many of these rulers were kings, princes, and landlords who had lost their power and influence as a result of British annexation and domination. They saw the rebellion as an opportunity to regain their lost status and to challenge the British authority.

In the beginning, most of the local rulers were hesitant to join the rebellion, as they were afraid of the consequences of challenging the mighty British Empire. However, as the rebellion spread, many of them saw an opportunity to reassert their authority and joined the rebel forces.

One of the most prominent local rulers who joined the rebellion was the last Mughal emperor, Bahadur Shah Zafar. He was a symbol of Indian sovereignty and was recognized as the nominal head of the rebellion. His involvement in the rebellion gave it a sense of legitimacy and unity.

Other local rulers who joined the rebellion included the Raja of Banaras, the Raja of Jhansi, the Nawab of Awadh, and the Nizam of Hyderabad. They all contributed men, money, and other resources to the rebel cause and played a crucial role in coordinating the rebellion.

The local rulers also used their influence and authority to mobilize the masses and create a sense of unity among the diverse groups of people. They used their networks and resources to spread the message of rebellion and to organize attacks on British military installations and other targets.

The involvement of the local rulers in the Indian Rebellion of 1857 was significant, as it provided the rebellion with a sense of legitimacy and authority. It also gave the rebellion a sense of direction and purpose, as the local rulers were able to coordinate the rebellion and provide leadership in the face of adversity. Although the rebellion was ultimately unsuccessful in overthrowing the British colonial authorities, the role played by the local rulers remains an important chapter in the history of the Indian freedom struggle.

4.2.5 Indian Soldiers

Indian soldiers played a significant role in the British army during the Indian Rebellion of 1857. They were known as sepoys and were recruited from various parts of India to serve in the British army. The sepoys were an integral part of the British military machine and were highly trained and disciplined soldiers.

At the time of the rebellion, there were over 300,000 sepoys in the British army, making up two-thirds of the entire force. They were responsible for maintaining law and order in the country and were often used to suppress rebellions and uprisings.

The sepoys had several grievances against the British authorities, including low pay, long hours, and discrimination. They were also unhappy with the introduction of new rifles, which used cartridges that were allegedly greased with pig and cow fat, which went against their religious beliefs.

The discontent among the sepoys eventually led to the outbreak of the Indian Rebellion of 1857, which saw many of them rise up against their British officers and refuse to use the new rifles. The sepoys were joined by civilians and other rebel forces, and together they launched a coordinated attack on British military installations and other targets.

Despite the large number of sepoys in the British army, many of them joined the rebel forces during the course of the rebellion. The rebels were able to win over the loyalty of the sepoys by appealing to their sense of national pride and their grievances against the British authorities.

The participation of the sepoys in the Indian Rebellion of 1857 was significant, as it showed that the Indian soldiers were not mere pawns in the British military machine but were capable of independent thought and action. Their participation in the rebellion also helped to galvanize support among the civilian population and other rebel forces, making it one of the largest and most widespread rebellions in Indian history.

4.2.6 Muslim and Hindu leaders

During the Indian Rebellion of 1857, both Muslim and Hindu leaders played a crucial role in mobilizing and leading the rebellion against the British. The rebellion was not just a military uprising but also a popular movement against British colonialism and exploitation, and it was led by a diverse group of leaders representing various communities and regions of India.

Hindu leaders such as Rani Lakshmibai of Jhansi, Tantia Tope, Nana Sahib, and Bahadur Shah Zafar were prominent figures in the rebellion. Rani Lakshmibai, also known as the "Queen of Jhansi," was a fierce warrior who led her troops into battle against the British. Tantia Tope was a military commander who led the rebellion in Central India, while Nana Sahib, the adopted son of the former Peshwa of the Maratha Empire, led the rebellion in the North. Bahadur Shah Zafar, the last Mughal emperor, was declared the leader of the rebellion and provided moral support to the rebel forces.

Muslim leaders such as Maulvi Ahmadullah, Maulvi Liaquat Ali, and Khan Bahadur Khan were also instrumental in the rebellion. Maulvi Ahmadullah, a charismatic Muslim cleric, led the rebellion in Awadh and was known for his fiery speeches and fearless leadership. Maulvi Liaquat Ali, another Muslim cleric, led the rebellion in Bihar and played a key role in mobilizing the Muslim peasantry. Khan Bahadur Khan, a Pashtun leader, led the rebellion in the North-West Frontier region and was known for his military prowess and strategic planning.

The participation of both Hindu and Muslim leaders in the rebellion showed that the rebellion was not limited to one community or region but was a pan-Indian movement against British rule. The leaders were able to mobilize support across religious and regional lines, and their participation gave the rebellion a sense of legitimacy and unity.

However, it is worth noting that the participation of both Hindu and Muslim leaders was not without tension and conflict. There were instances of communal violence and mistrust between the two communities, and some leaders prioritized their community's interests over the larger movement. Nonetheless, the participation of both Hindu and Muslim leaders in the rebellion remains a significant chapter in Indian history, highlighting the diverse and complex nature of the struggle against British colonialism.

4.3 The Unknown Faces Of Indian Rebellion of 1857

The Indian Rebellion of 1857, also known as the First War of Independence or the Sepoy Mutiny, was a watershed moment in Indian history. It was a mass uprising against British colonial rule that started with a mutiny among the sepoys (Indian soldiers) of the British East India Company and quickly spread to various parts of India. While the rebellion is often associated with the names of well-known leaders like Rani Lakshmibai, Nana Sahib, and Bahadur Shah Zafar, there were many others who participated in the rebellion and contributed to its success.

The rebellion was a popular movement that drew support from various sections of Indian society, including peasants, artisans, urban workers, and women. Many of these people, whose names and contributions are often forgotten or ignored, played an important role in the rebellion. They included local leaders, rebels, and ordinary people who were moved by the injustices of British colonial rule.

One example of an unknown face of the rebellion is Mangal Pandey's fellow sepoys, who also rebelled against the British. These sepoys came from various backgrounds and regions of India and fought bravely against the British. They were not always recognized for their contributions, and many were punished severely by the British when they were captured.

Another example is the ordinary people who provided support to the rebels. These included local villagers who provided food, shelter, and other necessities to the rebels, as well as women who smuggled weapons and ammunition for the rebels. These people risked their lives and faced punishment from the British when they were caught.

There were also rebel leaders who were not as well-known as Rani Lakshmibai or Nana Sahib but played a crucial role in the rebellion.

For example, Bakht Khan was a Muslim commander who led the rebellion in Delhi after Bahadur Shah Zafar was captured by the British. Bakht Khan and his forces fought bravely against the British and were able to hold off their attacks for several months.

The unknown faces of the Indian Rebellion of 1857 also include people who fought for causes that were not always recognized or acknowledged by the mainstream rebellion leadership. For example, there were rebels who fought against specific forms of British oppression, such as the imposition of taxes on local artisans or the destruction of religious sites. These rebels often acted independently or in small groups, and their contributions were not always recognized by the larger rebellion leadership.

In conclusion, the Indian Rebellion of 1857 was a complex and diverse movement that drew support from various sections of Indian society. While the well-known leaders played a significant role, there were many others who participated in the rebellion and contributed to its success. The contributions of these unknown faces of the rebellion highlight the diverse and decentralized nature of the struggle against British colonialism in India.

4.4 The Other Contributors

68

4.4.1 Bahadur Shah Zafar

Bahadur Shah Zafar was the last Mughal emperor of India and one of the key figures in the Indian Rebellion of 1857. He was born in 1775 in Delhi and was crowned emperor in 1837 at the age of 62.

Zafar was a poet and a Sufi who enjoyed a considerable reputation as a patron of the arts.

In the early 1850s, the British government passed a series of laws that further reduced the power and influence of the Mughal emperor. The laws also increased the political and economic oppression of the Indian people, which led to widespread discontent and opposition to the British.

In May 1857, a group of sepoys stationed in Meerut revolted against the British. The rebellion quickly spread throughout northern India, and Bahadur Shah Zafar was proclaimed the emperor of India by the rebels. Although Zafar was initially reluctant to join the rebellion, he eventually agreed to support it and became a symbol of Indian resistance to British colonial rule.

Zafar issued a proclamation calling for the overthrow of the British government and the restoration of Mughal power in India. He also issued coins and postage stamps in his name and appointed a council of leaders to assist him in the administration of his empire.

Zafar's support for the rebellion was critical in inspiring and mobilizing Indian soldiers and civilians to join the fight against the British. He became a rallying point for the rebels and was revered as a symbol of Indian unity and independence.

Despite his best efforts, the rebellion was eventually crushed by the British. Zafar was captured and exiled to Rangoon (now Yangon), where he lived out the rest of his life in relative obscurity. He died in 1862 at the age of 87.

Bahadur Shah Zafar's role in the Indian Rebellion of 1857 was significant in many ways. He was a symbol of Indian resistance to

British colonial rule and played a crucial role in inspiring and mobilizing Indian soldiers and civilians to join the rebellion. His contributions highlight the diverse and complex nature of the rebellion, and they demonstrate the important role that the Mughal emperor played in the fight for Indian independence.

4.4.2 Rani Lakshmibai

Rani Lakshmibai, also known as the Rani of Jhansi, was one of the key figures in the Indian Rebellion of

1857. She was born on 19 November 1835 in Varanasi, India. She was married to the Maharaja of Jhansi, Raja Gangadhar Rao, at a young age.

In 1853, the Maharaja passed away, leaving behind a young son and heir. The British government, however, refused to recognize the young boy as the rightful heir and annexed the state of Jhansi. This led to widespread anger and opposition among the local population, including Rani Lakshmibai.

In May 1857, the Indian Rebellion broke out, and Rani Lakshmibai took up arms against the British. She quickly emerged as a key leader in the rebellion, and her military skills and bravery earned her the respect of both her allies and enemies.

Under her leadership, the rebels launched a series of attacks on British forces in Jhansi and neighboring areas. She led her troops into battle herself and even adopted a son to ensure that the state of Jhansi would have an heir to the throne.

In June 1858, the British forces launched a major assault on Jhansi. Despite being outnumbered and outgunned, Rani Lakshmibai and her troops fought bravely and inflicted heavy losses on the British.

However, the British eventually managed to breach the defenses of Jhansi and capture the city.

Rani Lakshmibai managed to escape with her son and a group of loyal soldiers. She continued to lead her troops in a guerrilla war against the British, but in 1858, she was killed in battle in Gwalior.

Rani Lakshmibai's legacy in the Indian Rebellion of 1857 was significant. She is remembered as a symbol of Indian resistance to British colonial rule and as a fearless and inspiring leader who fought for the rights and independence of her people. Her contributions to the rebellion highlighted the role of women in the struggle for Indian independence, and she continues to inspire generations of Indians even today.

4.4.3 Nana Sahib

Nana Sahib, also known as Dhondu Pant, was one of the prominent leaders in the Indian Rebellion of 1857. He was born in 1824 in Bithoor, near Kanpur, India, and was the adopted son of Baji Rao II, the last Peshwa of the Maratha Empire.

After the British annexed the Maratha Empire, Nana Sahib's family lost their lands and wealth, and he became embittered towards the British. In 1853, his father died, and the British refused to recognize Nana Sahib's claim to his father's pension, which further fueled his anger and resentment towards the colonial rulers.

When the Indian Rebellion broke out in May 1857, Nana Sahib joined the rebel forces and became one of the key leaders of the rebellion in the north-central region of India. He played a critical role in the siege of Cawnpore (now Kanpur), where a large number of British civilians and soldiers were holed up.

In June 1857, the British forces agreed to a truce with the rebels and promised safe passage to the civilians and soldiers in Cawnpore in exchange for their surrender.

However, the British reneged on their promise, and instead, the rebels attacked the fleeing British forces. The incident became known as the Cawnpore Massacre, and Nana Sahib was blamed for ordering the killings.

After the Cawnpore Massacre, Nana Sahib went into hiding, and his whereabouts remained unknown for many years. He was rumored to have fled to Nepal or Tibet, but his fate remains a mystery to this day. Some reports suggest that he died in battle or was killed by the British, while others claim that he lived a long life in anonymity.

Nana Sahib's contributions to the Indian Rebellion of 1857 were significant. He was a charismatic leader who inspired many to take up arms against the British, and his role in the Cawnpore Massacre made him a controversial figure in Indian history. Even today, his story continues to fascinate and inspire Indians, and his legacy remains a subject of debate and discussion among historians and scholars.

4.4.4 Maulvi Ahmadullah

Maulvi Ahmadullah was a prominent figure in the Indian Rebellion of 1857. He was born in 1828 in the Faizabad district of Uttar Pradesh, India. Ahmadullah was a Muslim cleric who had studied in Mecca and Medina before returning to India to become a religious leader.

Ahmadullah was deeply committed to the cause of Indian independence and was an ardent critic of the British Raj. He traveled extensively throughout northern India, preaching the message of rebellion and encouraging people to rise up against British rule.

In May 1857, when the Indian Rebellion broke out, Ahmadullah played a critical role in organizing and leading the rebellion in the Awadh region. He led a group of rebels who captured the city of Faizabad and declared it as the capital of the new independent state of Awadh. Ahmadullah also played a key role in the siege of Lucknow and was instrumental in organizing the rebel forces.

Ahmadullah was known for his bravery and leadership skills, and he inspired many to join the rebellion against the British. However, his success was short-lived. In 1858, the British forces launched a major offensive against the rebel strongholds in Awadh, and Ahmadullah was forced to flee to Nepal. He was later captured by the British and sentenced to death.

Despite his capture and execution, Ahmadullah's legacy lived on. He became a symbol of resistance against British colonial rule and a source of inspiration for future generations of Indian nationalists. His story also highlights the critical role played by Muslim leaders in the Indian Rebellion of 1857, and their contributions to the struggle for Indian independence.

4.4.5 Bakht Khan

Bakht Khan was a prominent figure in the Indian Rebellion of 1857. He was born in 1797 in the Barabanki district of Uttar Pradesh, India. Bakht Khan was a soldier in the army of the last Mughal emperor, Bahadur Shah Zafar. He rose through the ranks to become one of the most trusted advisors of the emperor.

In May 1857, when the Indian Rebellion broke out, Bakht Khan played a critical role in organizing and leading the rebellion in Delhi. He led a group of soldiers who captured the Red Fort, which was the residence of the Mughal emperor. Bakht Khan then convinced the emperor to join the rebellion and declared him as the leader of the rebellion.

Under Bakht Khan's leadership, the rebel forces in Delhi were able to hold out against the British for several months. However, in September 1857, the British launched a major offensive against the rebel forces in Delhi, and Bakht Khan was forced to retreat to the city of Bareilly.

In Bareilly, Bakht Khan continued to lead the rebellion and was able to unite the rebel forces in the region. He formed an alliance with other rebel leaders, including Maulvi Ahmadullah and Nana Sahib, and fought a number of battles against the British.

Despite his efforts, the rebellion was eventually suppressed by the British in 1858. Bakht Khan was captured and sentenced to death, but his sentence was later commuted to life imprisonment.

Bakht Khan's story highlights the critical role played by soldiers in the Indian Rebellion of 1857, and their contributions to the struggle for Indian independence. He was a loyal soldier of the Mughal empire who became a key leader in the rebellion against British colonial rule. His legacy continues to inspire generations of Indians, and he is remembered as a hero of the Indian independence movement.

4.4.6 Tantia Tope

Tantia Tope was a prominent figure in the Indian Rebellion of 1857. He was born in 1814 in the village of Yeola in Maharashtra, India. Tantia Tope was a close associate of Nana Sahib, the adopted son of the last Peshwa of the Maratha Empire.

In May 1857, when the Indian Rebellion broke out, Tantia Tope joined the rebellion and played a critical role in organizing and leading the rebel forces. He fought a number of battles against the British, including the Siege of Jhansi and the Siege of Gwalior.

Tantia Tope's military skills and strategic planning were instrumental in the early successes of the rebellion. He was also known for his courage and determination, which earned him the respect and admiration of his fellow rebels.

Despite his military successes, Tantia Tope faced a number of setbacks in the later stages of the rebellion. In April 1859, he was captured by the British and was later tried and sentenced to death. He was hanged in April 1859 in Shivpuri, Madhya Pradesh.

Tantia Tope's story highlights the critical role played by military leaders in the Indian Rebellion of 1857, and their contributions to the struggle for Indian independence. He was a skilled general and a fearless fighter who dedicated his life to the cause of Indian independence. His legacy continues to inspire generations of Indians, and he is remembered as a hero of the Indian independence movement.

4.4.7 Maulvi Liaquat Ali

Maulvi Liaquat Ali was born in the mid-19th century in the city of Lucknow, India. He was a religious leader and scholar who had a large following among the local Muslim community. When the Indian Rebellion broke out in May 1857, Maulvi Liaquat Ali joined the rebels and became one of their key leaders.

Maulvi Liaquat Ali was instrumental in organizing and mobilizing the local Muslim community to join the rebellion. He was a charismatic figure who inspired his followers to take up arms against the British. He played a key role in the Siege of Lucknow, which lasted from June to November 1857.

During the siege, Maulvi Liaquat Ali was one of the chief commanders of the rebel forces. He was known for his tactical skills and bravery on the battlefield. He also provided religious and moral guidance to the rebels, helping to maintain their morale and commitment to the cause.

Despite the rebels' efforts, the Siege of Lucknow was eventually broken by the British. Maulvi Liaquat Ali was captured by the British and was later sentenced to death. He was executed in 1858, along with a number of other rebel leaders.

Maulvi Liaquat Ali's story highlights the role played by religious leaders in the Indian Rebellion of 1857. He was a respected figure in his community who used his position to rally support for the rebellion. His bravery and leadership continue to be remembered as a symbol of resistance against colonial rule.

4.4.8 Khan Bahadur Khan

Khan Bahadur Khan was a prominent figure in the Indian Rebellion of 1857. He was born in the district of Sitapur in the Awadh region of present-day Uttar Pradesh in India. He was a leader of the Pashtun community in the region and was known for his courage and military skills.

When the Indian Rebellion broke out in May 1857, Khan Bahadur Khan joined the rebellion and played a critical role in organizing and leading the rebel forces in the Awadh region. He led a successful rebellion against the British at the Battle of Chinhat, where he defeated a British force and captured their arms and ammunition.

Khan Bahadur Khan's military successes earned him a reputation as one of the most formidable rebel leaders in the region. He fought a number of battles against the British, including the Siege of Lucknow, where he led a group of rebels in defending the city against the British forces.

Despite his military successes, Khan Bahadur Khan faced a number of setbacks in the later stages of the rebellion. In March 1858, he was captured by the British and was later tried and sentenced to death.

He was hanged in April 1859 in Lucknow.

Khan Bahadur Khan's story highlights the critical role played by local leaders in the Indian Rebellion of 1857, and their contributions to the struggle for Indian independence. He was a skilled military leader and a fearless fighter who dedicated his life to the cause of Indian independence. His legacy continues to inspire generations of Indians, and he is remembered as a hero of the Indian independence movement

Chapter Five : Punjab's Patriotic Pioneers: Overlooked Contributors to India's Freedom Struggle

India's journey towards independence was a long and arduous one, marked by countless sacrifices, struggles, and heroic deeds. However, amidst the well-known names and stories of the freedom struggle, the role of Punjab's independence activists often goes unnoticed and unacknowledged. This book aims to shed light on the overlooked and undervalued contributions of Punjab's patriotic pioneers to India's quest for freedom.

From the 1857 rebellion to the Quit India Movement, Punjab's sons and daughters played an active and crucial role in various phases of India's struggle for independence. Yet, their sacrifices and contributions have not received the recognition they deserve. Through the pages of this book, we will explore the stories of some of these unsung heroes who dedicated their lives to the cause of a free India.

Their tales of courage, perseverance, and sacrifice will inspire and enlighten readers, revealing the hidden history of Punjab's independence movement. This book is an attempt to honor and pay tribute to the patriotic pioneers of Punjab who, despite facing immense challenges and hardships, never lost faith in their cause and continued their fight for freedom until the very end.

5.1 The Punjabi Warriors of Independence

Punjab, the land of five rivers, has a rich history of warriors and heroes who have fought bravely and sacrificed their lives for their land and people. The same spirit of courage and sacrifice was reflected in Punjab's role in India's freedom struggle. The Punjabi warriors of independence, as they are fondly remembered, played a crucial role in various phases of India's fight for freedom. This book is a tribute to their unyielding spirit and unwavering determination towards the cause of a free India.

Through the pages of this book, we will explore the inspiring stories of the Punjabi warriors of independence, who defied the might of the British Empire and stood up for their rights and dignity. From Bhagat Singh and Udham Singh to Lala Lajpat Rai and Kartar Singh Sarabha, we will delve into the lives and legacies of some of Punjab's most celebrated freedom fighters.

Their tales of courage and sacrifice, of standing up to oppression and injustice, will inspire and motivate readers, revealing the true meaning of patriotism and sacrifice. This book is a humble attempt to honor and pay tribute to the Punjabi warriors of independence, whose contributions to India's freedom struggle have often been overlooked and undervalued. Their legacy continues to inspire and guide us as we strive to build a just and equitable society for all.

5.1.1 Shaheed Bhagat Singh

Bhagat Singh was a prominent Indian socialist and revolutionary who played a pivotal role in India's fight for independence. He was born on September 28, 1907, in a small village called Banga in present-day Pakistan. His father, Kishan Singh, was a revolutionary activist who had been imprisoned for his involvement in the Ghadar conspiracy.

From a young age, Bhagat Singh was deeply influenced by his family's revolutionary legacy and was an avid reader of political and social literature. He was particularly inspired by the Russian Bolshevik revolution and the ideas of Karl Marx and Lenin.

In 1923, Bhagat Singh joined the National College in Lahore, where he became a member of the Hindustan Socialist Republican Association (HSRA). He was deeply committed to the cause of Indian independence and believed in the use of force to overthrow the British rule.

In 1928, Bhagat Singh and his comrades, Shivaram Rajguru and Sukhdev Thapar, were involved in the assassination of a British police officer, J.P. Saunders, who had been responsible for the brutal lathicharge on peaceful protesters. The trio went into hiding and were eventually arrested in April 1929.

Bhagat Singh's trial was a highly publicized event that attracted widespread attention and support for the independence movement. During the trial, Bhagat Singh and his co-accused used the court as a platform to propagate their revolutionary ideas and challenge the legitimacy of British rule.

On March 23, 1931, Bhagat Singh, Rajguru, and Sukhdev were sentenced to death for their involvement in the Saunders' murder. Despite a massive public outcry and widespread protests, the British government refused to commute their sentence.

On March 23, 1931, Bhagat Singh, Rajguru, and Sukhdev were hanged in the Lahore Central Jail. Their deaths sparked widespread outrage and further galvanized the independence movement.

Bhagat Singh's legacy continues to inspire generations of Indians and his name is synonymous with the struggle for freedom and justice. He was a firm believer in the principles of socialism and was deeply committed to creating a just and equitable society for all. His courage, determination, and sacrifice will always be remembered as a shining example of the spirit of Indian independence.

5.1.2 Lala Lajpat Rai

Lala Lajpat Rai, also known as Punjab Kesari (Lion of Punjab), was one of the most prominent leaders of India's independence movement. He was born on January 28, 1865, in a small town called Dhudike in present-day Punjab.

Lajpat Rai received his early education at the Government Higher Secondary School in Rewari and went on to study law at the Government College in Lahore. He was deeply influenced by the ideas of Swami Dayanand Saraswati and became an ardent advocate of social and religious reform.

In 1888, Lajpat Rai started his legal practice in Lahore, but soon became involved in social and political activism. He was one of the founders of the Indian National Congress and played a key role in the Swadeshi Movement, which aimed at promoting Indian-made goods and boycotting foreign goods.

Lajpat Rai was a strong advocate of Indian nationalism and believed in the use of non-violent means to achieve independence. He also played a crucial role in the formation of the All India Hindu Mahasabha, which aimed at promoting Hindu unity and protecting Hindu rights.

In 1928, Lajpat Rai led a procession against the Simon Commission, which had been appointed by the British government to review the functioning of the Indian government. The police responded with brutal force, and Lajpat Rai was severely beaten. He succumbed to his injuries on November 17, 1928, and his death sparked widespread outrage and protests across India.

Lajpat Rai's legacy continues to inspire generations of Indians, and his name is synonymous with the spirit of patriotism and sacrifice. He was a firm believer in the principles of democracy, freedom, and justice, and dedicated his life to the cause of Indian independence. His courage, determination, and sacrifice will always be remembered as a shining example of the spirit of Indian independence.

5.1.3 Dr. Bhim Rao Ambedkar

Dr. Bhim Rao Ambedkar, also known as Babasaheb Ambedkar, was one of the most prominent leaders of India's independence movement. He was born on April 14, 1891, in a small village called Mhow in present-day Madhya Pradesh.

Ambedkar belonged to the Dalit community, which was considered as untouchables in the Indian caste system. He faced severe discrimination and prejudice throughout his life, which shaped his commitment to social justice and equality.

Ambedkar was a brilliant scholar and received his education at Columbia University and the London School of Economics. He was deeply influenced by the ideas of John Dewey, a philosopher of education, and his doctoral thesis on the problem of the Indian rupee was a groundbreaking work in the field of economics.

Ambedkar was a strong advocate of political and social reform and worked tirelessly to uplift the Dalit community. He was one of the architects of the Indian Constitution and played a key role in drafting its provisions.

Ambedkar's contribution to the Indian independence movement was significant, and he was a staunch opponent of British colonial rule. He was a member of the Constituent Assembly and served as the first Law Minister of independent India.

Ambedkar's legacy continues to inspire generations of Indians, and his name is synonymous with the struggle for social justice and equality. He was a firm believer in the principles of democracy, freedom, and justice, and dedicated his life to the cause of Indian independence. His courage, determination, and sacrifice will always be remembered as a shining example of the spirit of Indian independence.

5.1.4 Maulana Azad

Maulana Abul Kalam Azad was one of the most prominent leaders of India's independence movement.

He was born on November 11, 1888, in Mecca, which is now in Saudi Arabia.

Azad was a scholar and a prolific writer, and he was deeply committed to the cause of Indian independence. He was also a prominent leader of the Indian National Congress and served as its president from 1940 to 1945.

Azad was a strong advocate of Hindu-Muslim unity and believed in the need for India to be a secular state. He worked tirelessly to bridge the divide between the two communities and was instrumental in the formation of the Jamia Millia Islamia University, which aimed at promoting education and social reform among Muslims.

Azad's contribution to the Indian independence movement was significant, and he played a key role in negotiating the transfer of power from the British to the Indian government. He served as the Minister of Education in independent India and worked to promote education and social reform.

Azad's legacy continues to inspire generations of Indians, and his name is synonymous with the spirit of patriotism and sacrifice. He was a firm believer in the principles of democracy, freedom, and justice, and dedicated his life to the cause of Indian independence. His courage, determination, and sacrifice will always be remembered as a shining example of the spirit of Indian independence.

5.1.5 Sarojini Naidu

Sarojini Naidu was a prominent leader of India's independence movement and one of the most influential women of her time. She was born on February 13, 1879, in Hyderabad, India, and was fondly known as the "Nightingale of India" for her poetry and oratory skills.

Naidu was a gifted writer and a passionate social reformer who dedicated her life to the cause of Indian independence. She was a close associate of Mahatma Gandhi and played a significant role in mobilizing women in the freedom struggle. She was the first woman to be elected as the President of the Indian National Congress.

Naidu was a staunch advocate of women's rights and worked tirelessly to promote education and social reform. She was a member of the Constituent Assembly and played a key role in drafting the Indian Constitution.

Naidu's contribution to the Indian independence movement was significant, and she was a prominent voice in the struggle for freedom. Her speeches and writings inspired generations of Indians, and she was a symbol of the courage and determination of the Indian people.

Naidu's legacy continues to inspire women across the world, and her name is synonymous with the spirit of patriotism and sacrifice. She was a firm believer in the principles of democracy, freedom, and justice, and dedicated her life to the cause of Indian independence. Her courage, determination, and sacrifice will always be remembered as a shining example of the spirit of Indian independence.

5.1.6 Kartar Singh Sarabha

Kartar Singh Sarabha was a revolutionary and a prominent leader of India's independence movement. He was born on May 24, 1896, in Sarabha village, Punjab.

Sarabha was deeply influenced by the ideas of Bhagat Singh and joined the Hindustan Socialist

Republican Association (HSRA), a revolutionary organization that aimed at overthrowing British colonial rule in India. He played a key role in the Lahore conspiracy case of 1915, which was one of the most significant trials in the Indian independence movement.

Sarabha was a brilliant scholar and received his education in the United States, where he became involved with the Ghadar Party, a revolutionary group that aimed at overthrowing British rule in India. He returned to India in 1914 and joined the HSRA, where he became a close associate of Bhagat Singh.

Sarabha was one of the masterminds of the HSRA's plan to bomb the Central Legislative Assembly in Delhi in 1929. The plan was intended to be a wake-up call to the British and to inspire the Indian people to rise up against colonial rule. However, the plan was foiled, and Sarabha and his comrades were arrested and sentenced to death.

Sarabha's sacrifice and commitment to the cause of Indian independence inspired generations of Indians, and his name is synonymous with the spirit of patriotism and sacrifice. He was a firm believer in the principles of democracy, freedom, and justice, and dedicated his life to the cause of Indian independence.

Sarabha's legacy continues to inspire revolutionaries and freedom fighters across the world. He was a symbol of the courage, determination, and sacrifice of the Indian people, and his memory will always be remembered as a shining example of the spirit of Indian independence.

5.1.7 Bhai Parmanand

Bhai Parmanand was a revolutionary and a prominent leader of India's independence movement. He was born on July 5, 1876, in the Jhelum district of Punjab.

Bhai Parmanand was a gifted writer and an eloquent orator who used his skills to mobilize the masses in the struggle for Indian independence. He was a close associate of Lala Lajpat Rai and played a key role in organizing the protests against the Simon Commission.

Bhai Parmanand was a staunch advocate of the rights of the Indian people and worked tirelessly to promote social reform and education. He was a member of the All India Congress Committee and played a key role in drafting the Indian National Congress's constitution.

Bhai Parmanand's contribution to the Indian independence movement was significant, and he was a prominent voice in the struggle for freedom. His speeches and writings inspired generations of Indians, and he was a symbol of the courage and determination of the Indian people.

Bhai Parmanand's legacy continues to inspire freedom fighters and activists across the world. He was a firm believer in the principles of democracy, freedom, and justice, and dedicated his life to the cause of Indian independence. His courage, determination, and sacrifice will always be remembered as a shining example of the spirit of Indian independence.

5.1.8 Baba Kharak Singh

Baba Kharak Singh was a prominent leader of the Indian independence movement and a revered figure in the Sikh community. He was born on February 6, 1868, in a village in the Rawalpindi district of Punjab. Baba Kharak Singh was a visionary leader who was deeply committed to the cause of Indian independence. He was an ardent nationalist who believed in the principles of freedom, democracy, and justice. He was a member of the Indian National Congress and played a key role in the struggle for Indian independence.

Baba Kharak Singh was a passionate advocate for the rights of the Sikh community and worked tirelessly to promote their interests. He was a strong proponent of Sikh education and was instrumental in the establishment of the Khalsa College in Amritsar.

Baba Kharak Singh was a vocal critic of the British colonial rule in India and participated in several protests and demonstrations against the British. He was also a prominent figure in the Non-Cooperation Movement launched by Mahatma Gandhi in 1920 and played a key role in organizing the boycott of foreign goods.

Baba Kharak Singh was a firm believer in the power of non-violent resistance, but he was also a strong advocate for the use of force when necessary. He was a close associate of Bhagat Singh and played a key role in the Hindustan Socialist Republican Association.

Baba Kharak Singh's leadership and commitment to the cause of Indian independence inspired generations of Indians, and his name is synonymous with the spirit of patriotism and sacrifice. He was a symbol of the courage, determination, and sacrifice of the Indian people, and his memory will always be remembered as a shining example of the spirit of Indian independence.

Baba Kharak Singh's legacy continues to inspire freedom fighters and activists across the world. He was a visionary leader who believed in the principles of democracy, freedom, and justice, and dedicated his life to the cause of Indian independence. His courage, determination, and sacrifice will always be remembered as a shining example of the spirit of Indian independence.

5.1.9 Giani Zail Singh

Giani Zail Singh was a prominent political figure and a dedicated leader of the Indian National Congress.

He was born on May 5, 1916, in Sandhwan, a village in the present-day Punjab state of India.

Giani Zail Singh was an active participant in the Indian independence movement and was deeply committed to the cause of Indian independence. He joined the Indian National Congress at a young age and worked closely with Jawaharlal Nehru and other leaders in the struggle for Indian independence. After India gained independence, Giani Zail Singh was appointed as a member of the Punjab Legislative

Assembly and served as a cabinet minister in the Punjab government. He was also elected as the Speaker of the Punjab Legislative Assembly and later served as the Chief Minister of Punjab.

In 1982, Giani Zail Singh was elected as the President of India, the highest office in the country. As President, he worked to promote the principles of democracy, freedom, and justice and played a key role in the country's political and social development.

Giani Zail Singh was a strong advocate for the rights of the poor and marginalized sections of society and worked tirelessly to promote their interests. He was also a vocal critic of the abuse of power and corruption in politics and worked to promote transparency and accountability in government. Giani Zail Singh's contribution to the Indian independence movement and the country's political and social development was significant. He was a prominent voice in the struggle for freedom and dedicated his life to the service of the Indian people. His legacy continues to inspire generations of Indians, and his memory is honored as a symbol of the country's rich cultural heritage and the spirit of patriotism and sacrifice.

5.1.10 Satyapal Dang

Satyapal Dang was an Indian politician and freedom fighter who played a significant role in the struggle for Indian independence. He was born on June 7, 1920, in Dang village in present-day Haryana, India. Satyapal Dang was deeply influenced by the Indian independence movement from a young age and was an active participant in it. He joined the Indian National Congress at a young age and worked closely with other leaders of the freedom struggle, including Mahatma Gandhi and Jawaharlal Nehru. Dang was a dedicated follower of the Gandhian philosophy of non-violence and civil disobedience. He was involved in many peaceful protests and demonstrations against the British colonial rule and was arrested and jailed several times for his activism.

During the Quit India Movement of 1942, Satyapal Dang led a group of young freedom fighters in his village and organized a mass protest against the British colonial rule. As a result of this, he was arrested and sentenced to prison.

After India gained independence, Satyapal Dang continued to work for the development of the country and was elected to the Lok Sabha, the lower house of the Indian Parliament. He served as a member of Parliament for many years and played a key role in the development of his constituency and the country as a whole.

In addition to his political career, Satyapal Dang was also a prominent social worker and worked to promote education, healthcare, and social welfare programs in his community. He founded several charitable organizations and institutions that continue to provide essential services to the people of his constituency.

Satyapal Dang's contribution to the Indian independence movement and his work for the development of the country were significant. He was a dedicated leader and a tireless worker for the welfare of the people, and his legacy continues to inspire generations of Indians to this day.

5.1.11 Master Tara Singh

Master Tara Singh was a prominent Sikh political leader who played a significant role in India's struggle for independence from British rule. Born on June 24, 1885, in Rawalpindi, now in Pakistan, he was a staunch advocate of the rights of the Sikh community and worked tirelessly to promote their interests. Master Tara Singh started his political career as a member of the Indian National Congress, but later became disillusioned with the party's lack of focus on Sikh issues. He then became a member of the Shiromani Akali Dal, a political party that worked to promote the interests of the Sikh community. In 1920, Master Tara Singh became a member of the Punjab Legislative Council and worked to pass laws that would benefit the Sikh community. He also became involved in the Akali movement, which sought to reform the management of Sikh temples, known as gurdwaras. In 1925, he became the president of the Shiromani Gurdwara Prabandhak Committee (SGPC), which is responsible for the management of gurdwaras in Punjab.

In 1940, Master Tara Singh played a leading role in the Lahore Resolution, which called for the creation of a separate Muslim state in India. However, he later became an ardent opponent of the partition of India, which resulted in the formation of Pakistan. He believed that the partition would be detrimental to the interests of the Sikh community and would lead to their marginalization.

During the partition, Master Tara Singh led the demand for the creation of a separate Sikh state, known as Khalistan. However, his demand was not accepted by the Indian government, and he was arrested for his involvement in the movement. He was released in 1949 and continued to work for the rights of the Sikh community.

Master Tara Singh was a strong supporter of the Punjabi language and worked to promote its use in education and government. He believed that the promotion of Punjabi would help to strengthen the cultural identity of the Sikh community and would give them a sense of pride in their heritage. Master Tara Singh's contribution to India's struggle for independence was significant, and his legacy continues to inspire many people in India and around the world. He was a visionary leader who worked tirelessly for the rights of the Sikh community and the promotion of Punjabi language and culture. His ideas and philosophy continue to shape Indian society and politics to this day.

5.1.12 Sahib Singh Verma

Sahib Singh Verma (1943-2007) was an Indian politician and a prominent leader of the Bharatiya Janata Party (BJP) in Delhi. He was the Chief Minister of Delhi from 1996 to 1998 and played an active role in the Indian independence movement. Here is a brief overview of his life and contributions to India's struggle for independence.

Sahib Singh Verma was born on 15 May 1943 in Delhi. He was the son of Shri Udai Singh Verma, a prominent leader of the Indian National Congress. Verma completed his early education at a local school in Delhi and later pursued higher studies at the University of Delhi. During his student days, he became involved in the Indian independence movement and joined the Akhil Bharatiya Vidyarthi Parishad (ABVP), the student wing of the Rashtriya Swayamsevak Sangh (RSS).

In 1977, Verma contested the Delhi Legislative Assembly elections as a candidate of the Janata Party and won from the Mehrauli constituency. He was subsequently re-elected from the same constituency in

1980, 1983, and 1985. During this period, he played an active role in various social and political movements and was associated with several organizations, including the Vishva Hindu Parishad and the Bajrang Dal.

Verma's commitment to the cause of Indian nationalism and his support for the BJP's ideology of

Hindutva led to his appointment as the Chief Minister of Delhi in 1996. During his tenure, he initiated several development projects, including the construction of flyovers, parks, and other public amenities.

He also introduced measures to improve the law and order situation in the city.

Apart from his administrative and political contributions, Verma was also a prolific writer and social activist. He wrote several books on Indian politics, culture, and religion and was a vocal advocate for the rights of the marginalized sections of society.

In conclusion, Sahib Singh Verma was a prominent political leader who played a significant role in India's struggle for independence. His commitment to the ideals of Indian nationalism and his contributions to the development of Delhi will always be remembered.

5.1.13 Madan Lal Dhingra

Madan Lal Dhingra was an Indian revolutionary who is best known for assassinating Sir William Hutt Curzon Wyllie, a British official, in London in 1909. His actions sparked a renewed fervor for Indian independence and inspired many other young Indians to join the struggle.

Dhingra was born in Amritsar in 1883, the son of a wealthy Hindu family. He received his early education at Amritsar and later moved to Lahore where he studied engineering at the Government College. It was at Lahore that he became interested in politics and was exposed to the ideas of the Indian National Congress and the revolutionary movement.

In 1905, Dhingra went to England to study mechanical engineering at University College, London. There he became involved with the Indian Independence movement and the activities of the Indian Sociologist, an organization of Indian students in London that aimed to support the cause of Indian independence. Dhingra also became associated with the revolutionary group, Abhinav Bharat, and began to advocate the use of violence to achieve Indian independence.

Dhingra's moment of fame came on July 1, 1909, when he assassinated Sir William Hutt Curzon Wyllie, a prominent British official, at a meeting of the Indian National Association in London. He was immediately arrested and charged with murder. During his trial, Dhingra made a speech in which he proclaimed that he was not a terrorist but a patriot and that his actions were a direct response to the injustices perpetrated by the British in India. He was found guilty and sentenced to death.

Dhingra's execution on August 17, 1909, caused a sensation in India and became a rallying cry for the

Indian Independence movement. His actions were widely celebrated as a brave and heroic act of resistance against British colonialism. His death also led to an increase in support for the revolutionary movement and a growing sense of nationalism among the Indian people.

Today, Madan Lal Dhingra is remembered as a symbol of the Indian Independence movement and a hero of Indian nationalism. His assassination of Sir William Hutt Curzon Wyllie is seen as a significant event in the struggle for Indian independence and a testament to the courage and sacrifice of those who fought for their country's freedom.

5.1.14 Bhagat Puran Singh

Bhagat Puran Singh was a visionary and selfless leader who dedicated his life to serving the underprivileged and marginalized sections of society. He was born on June 4, 1904, in a small village named Rajewal, near Amritsar, Punjab. He grew up in poverty but was highly motivated to pursue education, which he saw as the key to improving his and his community's life.

In 1929, Bhagat Puran Singh completed his degree in Physical Science from Khalsa College, Amritsar. However, instead of pursuing a lucrative career, he decided to devote his life to social service. He started working as a medical assistant in Amritsar and treated patients for free. He believed that healthcare should be a basic right, and nobody should be denied medical treatment due to their financial situation. In 1947, when India gained independence, the partition of the country led to widespread violence and displacement. Bhagat Puran Singh witnessed the suffering of the people, and he decided to help the refugees. He started an organization called Pingalwara, which means "a home for the disabled," in Amritsar in 1948. The organization provided free food, shelter, and medical care to the homeless, destitute, and disabled people.

Bhagat Puran Singh worked tirelessly to expand Pingalwara's services. He personally went out to the streets to find the homeless and disabled people and brought them to Pingalwara. He also inspired others to join him in his mission of service. Under his leadership, Pingalwara grew into a vast network of institutions that provided care and support to people with disabilities.

In addition to Pingalwara, Bhagat Puran Singh also started a project called "Guru ka Langar," which provided free food to the poor and needy. He believed that no one should go hungry, and it was the responsibility of the society to provide food to those who couldn't afford it.

Bhagat Puran Singh was a man of great humility and kindness. He believed that serving others was the true purpose of life, and he lived his life in service to others. He received many awards and honors for his work, including the Padma Shri award in 1979, but he remained humble and continued to work tirelessly for the betterment of society.

Bhagat Puran Singh passed away on August 5, 1992, but his legacy lives on. Pingalwara continues to provide free healthcare, food, and shelter to the underprivileged, and it has become an inspiration for many others who want to serve society. Bhagat Puran Singh's life is a testament to the power of selflessness and service, and he will always be remembered as a true hero of India's independence struggle.

5.1.15 Dr. Mulk Raj Anand

Dr. Mulk Raj Anand was an important figure in Indian literature, known for his powerful and poignant writing that often addressed themes of social inequality and injustice. Born in Peshawar in 1905, he grew up in Amritsar and Lahore, and was deeply influenced by the nationalist movement for Indian independence. His experiences of witnessing poverty, discrimination, and violence against marginalized communities, particularly the Dalits or untouchables, shaped his worldview and his writing.

Anand's literary career began in the 1930s with the publication of his first novel, "Untouchable", which is widely considered a classic of modern Indian literature. The novel tells the story of a day in the life of a young Dalit boy named Bakha, who is forced to work as a latrine cleaner and is shunned by society. Anand's vivid and powerful depiction of Bakha's struggles and his attempts to assert his humanity in the face of prejudice and oppression resonated with readers across India and beyond, and helped to bring issues of caste discrimination and social justice to the forefront of the national discourse.

Throughout his career, Anand continued to write about social and political issues, and his work often addressed themes of poverty, class, and injustice. He was a strong advocate for the rights of the marginalized, and was deeply involved in social and political movements aimed at promoting greater equality and justice in Indian society. He was an active member of the Indian People's Theatre Association, and worked with other artists and writers to use their craft as a tool for social change.

Anand's commitment to social justice was reflected not only in his writing, but also in his personal life. He was involved in various progressive movements and worked closely with leaders of the Indian independence movement, including Mahatma Gandhi and Jawaharlal Nehru. He also helped to found the Progressive Writers' Association, which brought together writers from across India who shared a commitment to social and political change.

Anand's literary career spanned several decades, and he was the recipient of numerous awards and honors for his work. He was also a respected teacher and scholar, and taught at universities in India, Europe, and the United States. His writing and his activism had a profound impact on Indian literature and on the social and political movements of his time, and his legacy continues to inspire writers and activists to this day.

In conclusion, Dr. Mulk Raj Anand was a prolific and influential writer who used his work to shed light on social inequality and injustice. He was a passionate advocate for the rights of the marginalized, and his writing and his activism helped to bring important social and political issues to the forefront of public consciousness. His legacy continues to be celebrated and honored by readers and writers around the world, and his contributions to Indian literature and to the struggle for social justice will never be forgotten.

5.1.16 Faiz Ahmad Faiz

Faiz Ahmad Faiz was a renowned Pakistani poet and writer, known for his contributions to Urdu literature and his activism for social justice and human rights. He was born on February 13, 1911, in Kala Qader, Punjab, British India. Faiz belonged to a family of intellectuals and was well-educated. He completed his education at the Government College University in Lahore, where he was influenced by the leftist ideas of the time.

Faiz began his career as a teacher, but his passion for writing soon led him to work as an editor for various newspapers and literary magazines. He wrote poetry that was both lyrical and political, using his art to express the struggles of the common people and to challenge the injustices of the ruling classes.

His poetry often addressed themes of revolution, freedom, and social justice.

Faiz was a member of the Communist Party of Pakistan and actively supported various progressive and leftist causes. He was imprisoned several times for his activism, including during the Indian independence movement and later, during the dictatorship of General Zia-ul-Haq. During his imprisonment, he wrote some of his most famous poems, which were later compiled into a book called "Zindan Nama" (The Prison Letters).

Faiz was a prolific writer, and his works include poetry, essays, and translations. His poetry has been translated into many languages and has earned him a place among the most celebrated poets of the twentieth century. Some of his most famous works include "Dast-e-Saba," "Shaam-e-Firaq Ab Na Puch," and "Mujh Se Pehli Si Mohabbat."

In addition to his literary achievements, Faiz was also an important political figure in Pakistan. He served as the editor of the daily newspaper "Pakistan Times" and was a member of the National

Assembly of Pakistan. He was awarded numerous honors for his contributions to literature and social justice, including the Lenin Peace Prize and the Nishan-e-Imtiaz, Pakistan's highest civilian award.

Faiz Ahmad Faiz passed away on November 20, 1984, in Lahore, Pakistan. He left behind a legacy of poetry and activism that continues to inspire people around the world. His works continue to be studied and celebrated as a symbol of resistance against injustice and oppression.

5.1.17 Bhai Randhir Singh

Bhai Randhir Singh was a prominent Sikh revolutionary who played a significant role in the Indian independence movement. Born on 7 July 1878 in the Punjab province, Bhai Randhir Singh was an active member of the Ghadar Party, a revolutionary organization established in the United States that aimed to overthrow British rule in India. He was also an ardent follower of the Sikh religion and worked tirelessly to promote its principles and values.

Bhai Randhir Singh became involved in the Indian independence movement during his studies in Lahore, where he was a member of the Indian National Congress. However, he soon became disillusioned with the party's non-violent approach and turned to more radical means of resistance. In 1914, he was arrested for his involvement in the Ghadar conspiracy and was sentenced to life imprisonment.

Despite being imprisoned, Bhai Randhir Singh continued to be a strong advocate for India's freedom and the Sikh religion. He wrote several books on the Sikh faith and became an influential figure among the Sikh community. He also played a key role in the Akali movement, which aimed to reform the management of Sikh shrines and temples.

In 1920, Bhai Randhir Singh was released from prison following a general amnesty. He returned to his home village and continued his work in promoting the Sikh religion and supporting the independence movement. He was a close associate of other Indian freedom fighters, such as Bhagat Singh and Lala Lajpat Rai.

In 1929, Bhai Randhir Singh was arrested once again for his involvement in the Indian independence movement. He was sentenced to several years of imprisonment, during which time he continued to write and inspire others with his words. He was finally released in 1931 and continued to work towards the cause of Indian independence until his death in 1961.

Bhai Randhir Singh's life and work continue to be an inspiration to many. He remains a beloved figure among the Sikh community and is remembered for his unwavering commitment to the cause of India's freedom and the Sikh religion. His books and writings continue to be widely read and his legacy continues to influence those who seek to make a positive impact on the world.

In conclusion, Bhai Randhir Singh was a remarkable individual who played a vital role in the Indian independence movement. His unwavering commitment to the cause of India's freedom and the Sikh religion inspired many, and his legacy continues to be celebrated to this day. His life and work serve as an example of the power of dedication, perseverance, and faith in making a positive difference in the world.

5.1.18 Kartar Singh Jhabbar

Kartar Singh Jhabbar was an Indian revolutionary and freedom fighter who played an important role in

India's struggle for independence. Born in 1901 in the village of Jhabbar in Punjab, Kartar Singh was deeply influenced by the teachings of Bhagat Singh and became an active participant in the Indian nationalist movement during the 1920s and 30s.

Kartar Singh joined the Indian National Congress in 1923 and quickly became known for his fiery speeches and aggressive approach towards the British authorities. He also became involved in the Ghadar Party, a revolutionary group that aimed to overthrow British rule in India through armed struggle.

Kartar Singh was arrested several times for his political activities and spent a total of 14 years in prison.

In 1929, Kartar Singh was one of the leaders of the Kirti Kisan movement, which fought for the rights of farmers and agricultural workers in Punjab. The movement gained widespread support and was successful in achieving some of its goals, such as reducing land rent and improving working conditions.

During the Quit India movement of 1942, Kartar Singh played a prominent role in organizing protests and agitations against British rule. He was arrested once again and sentenced to life imprisonment, which he served in several different prisons across India.

After India gained independence in 1947, Kartar Singh continued to be involved in politics and social activism. He became a member of the Punjab Legislative Assembly and worked to improve the lives of farmers and laborers. He also founded the Kisan Mazdoor Khudkushi Peedit Parivar Committee, an organization that provided support and assistance to families affected by farmer suicides in Punjab.

Kartar Singh Jhabbar was a committed socialist and believed in the power of collective action to bring about social change. He saw the struggle for India's independence as part of a larger global struggle for freedom and justice. He passed away in 1975, but his legacy as a fearless and dedicated freedom fighter lives on.

In conclusion, Kartar Singh Jhabbar was a prominent figure in India's independence movement and dedicated his life to fighting for the rights of farmers, laborers, and oppressed communities. He faced imprisonment and persecution but remained committed to his principles and the cause of freedom. His contributions to the struggle for independence and social justice continue to inspire generations of activists and revolutionaries.

5.1.19 Dr. Satyapal

Dr. Satyapal was a prominent Indian nationalist and political leader who played a significant role in the Indian independence movement. Born in Punjab in July 1882, he was a highly educated individual with a deep commitment to social justice and political freedom. His contribution to the Indian independence movement was immense, and he played a pivotal role in the formation of the All India Scheduled Castes Federation, which fought for the rights of the Dalits and other marginalized sections of society. Dr. Satyapal was a graduate of the King Edward Medical College in Lahore and practiced medicine for some time before entering politics. He was a strong advocate of Indian nationalism and opposed British colonialism in India. He was an active member of the Indian National Congress and played a leading role in the Non-Cooperation Movement launched by Mahatma Gandhi in 1920. In fact, he was one of the main organizers of the movement in the Punjab region and played a significant role in mobilizing the masses.

Dr. Satyapal's political activism was not limited to the Congress. He was a member of the Shiromani Akali Dal, a political party that represented the Sikh community in Punjab. He was deeply committed to the cause of Dalit rights and worked closely with Bhimrao Ambedkar, the leader of the Dalit movement in India. Together, they founded the All India Scheduled Castes Federation, which fought for the rights of Dalits and other marginalized communities.

In 1922, Dr. Satyapal was arrested and imprisoned by the British colonial authorities for his involvement in the Non-Cooperation Movement. His arrest sparked a massive protest in the Punjab region, and the people of Punjab came out on the streets to demand his release. The protest turned violent, and the British authorities responded with brute force. The Jallianwala Bagh Massacre, in which hundreds of unarmed civilians were killed by British troops, took place in the aftermath of the protest.

Despite the repression and violence of the colonial authorities, Dr. Satyapal remained committed to the cause of Indian independence. He was elected to the Punjab Legislative Council in 1923 and continued to play an active role in politics. In 1929, he was elected as the President of the Punjab Provincial Congress Committee and worked closely with other leaders such as Lala Lajpat Rai and Jawaharlal Nehru to organize the Civil Disobedience Movement in Punjab.

Dr. Satyapal's contribution to the Indian independence movement was immense, and he remained a strong advocate of social justice and political freedom throughout his life. He passed away in 1947, just before India achieved independence, but his legacy lives on. He continues to inspire generations of Indians with his courage, commitment, and dedication to the cause of Indian independence and social justice.

5.1.20 Dr. Saifuddin Kitchlew Satyapal

Dr. Saifuddin Kitchlew Satyapal was an Indian nationalist and a prominent leader of the Indian independence movement. He was born on January 15, 1888, in Amritsar, Punjab. He was a physician by profession and had earned a medical degree from the King Edward Medical College, Lahore. Dr. Satyapal was deeply influenced by the Indian nationalist movement and became actively involved in it.

Dr. Satyapal's political activism started in 1914 when he joined the Indian National Congress. He became a close associate of Mahatma Gandhi and actively participated in the Non-Cooperation Movement in 1920. He was elected as the President of the Punjab Congress Committee in 1921.

In 1919, the British government passed the Rowlatt Act, which authorized the government to detain individuals without trial and restricted civil liberties. This act was met with widespread protests and strikes across India. In Punjab, the agitation was particularly strong, and Dr. Satyapal played a leading role in the protests.

On April 10, 1919, a massive protest meeting was held in Jallianwala Bagh in Amritsar to protest against the Rowlatt Act. The meeting was peaceful, but it was declared illegal by the British authorities, and General Dyer ordered his troops to open fire on the unarmed crowd. The firing continued for about ten minutes, resulting in the death of over 1,000 people and leaving over 1,500 wounded.

Dr. Satyapal and Dr. Saifuddin Kitchlew, another prominent leader of the Indian National Congress, were arrested on April 9, 1919, by the British authorities in response to the protests. Their arrest sparked widespread outrage and further protests across India.

After their release, Dr. Satyapal continued to be actively involved in the Indian nationalist movement. He was arrested several times for his participation in various protests and movements. He was arrested again in 1942 during the Quit India Movement, which demanded the immediate end of British rule in India. Dr. Satyapal, along with other nationalist leaders, was kept in prison until India gained independence in 1947.

In independent India, Dr. Satyapal continued to serve the people as a member of the Constituent Assembly and later as a Member of Parliament. He remained committed to the cause of social justice and fought against communalism, untouchability, and other social evils.

Dr. Satyapal's contribution to the Indian independence movement is significant. He played a prominent role in the Jallianwala Bagh massacre, which is considered a turning point in India's struggle for independence. He continued to be an active participant in various movements and protests until India gained independence. He remained committed to the cause of social justice and dedicated his life to the service of the people of India.

5.1.21 Giani Ditt Singh

Giani Ditt Singh was a prominent Sikh intellectual, scholar, and reformer who played an important role in India's independence movement. He was born in 1850 in the village of Bhadur, which is now located in the Ludhiana district of Punjab. From a young age, Giani Ditt Singh was passionate about education and spent much of his time reading and studying.

Giani Ditt Singh was a firm believer in the idea of social reform and spent much of his life working to promote equality and justice for all. He was particularly concerned about the position of women in society and was a strong advocate for their rights. He also worked to promote education, especially for the poor and marginalized communities.

Giani Ditt Singh was an ardent supporter of the Indian independence movement and was involved in various political and social movements. He was a close associate of the great Sikh reformer, Bhai Maharaj Singh, and played an active role in the Kuka movement, which sought to establish a Sikh state in the Punjab.

In 1906, Giani Ditt Singh was elected as the president of the All India Anti-Caste Association, a position he held for several years. He was also involved in the Indian National Congress and actively supported the non-cooperation movement launched by Mahatma Gandhi in 1920.

Giani Ditt Singh was a prolific writer and wrote extensively on a variety of topics, including religion, politics, and social reform. He was the author of several books, including "Sikhism and Social Reform," "The Sikh Religion: Its Gurus, Sacred Writings, and Authors," and "The Indian Struggle for Freedom." Despite his many contributions to Indian society, Giani Ditt Singh was not immune to persecution. He was arrested and imprisoned several times for his involvement in various political and social movements. In 1921, he was arrested for his participation in the non-cooperation movement and spent several months in prison.

Giani Ditt Singh passed away in 1927, leaving behind a legacy of social and political activism that continues to inspire people to this day. He was a tireless champion of the oppressed and marginalized, and his work played a significant role in shaping the social and political landscape of India in the years leading up to its independence

5.1.22 Master Sunder Singh Lyallpuri

Master Sunder Singh Lyallpuri was a prominent figure in the Indian independence movement, particularly in the Punjab region. He was born on February 5, 1885, in the Lyallpur district of Punjab (now in Pakistan). Lyallpuri was a school teacher by profession and had a deep interest in politics and social reform. He played a crucial role in shaping the political landscape of Punjab during the struggle for independence.

Lyallpuri was heavily influenced by the Ghadar movement, which sought to overthrow British rule in India. He participated in various protests and rallies organized by the movement, and was even arrested and imprisoned for his involvement. Later, he became associated with the Indian National Congress and served as the president of the Punjab Congress Committee.

In 1929, Lyallpuri led the Salt Satyagraha movement in the Punjab region, which aimed to protest against the British salt tax. He led a group of protesters to the Ravi River, where they defied the salt laws by making salt from seawater. The protest was met with violent repression by the British authorities, and Lyallpuri was arrested along with other leaders of the movement.

Lyallpuri was also a vocal advocate for the rights of the Sikh community in Punjab. He fought for the recognition of the Punjabi language and campaigned for the establishment of Punjabi-language schools.

He was a staunch opponent of the caste system and worked towards promoting social equality.

During the partition of India in 1947, Lyallpuri was a vocal critic of the idea of dividing Punjab on religious lines. He believed that such a division would lead to violence and suffering for both Hindus and Muslims.

Despite his efforts to prevent the partition, Punjab was ultimately divided, leading to the displacement of millions of people and widespread violence.

Lyallpuri continued to work for the betterment of society until his death on October 23, 1948. He was a passionate advocate for social justice and a tireless fighter for the rights of the oppressed. His legacy lives on as a testament to the courage and determination of those who fought for India's independence. In conclusion, Master Sunder Singh Lyallpuri was a prominent figure in the Indian independence movement, who fought for the rights of the oppressed and worked towards promoting social equality. His leadership in the Salt Satyagraha movement and his advocacy for the Punjabi language and the Sikh community in Punjab made him a beloved and respected figure in the region. His legacy as a champion of social justice continues to inspire generations of Indians

5.1.23 Sardar Ajit Singh

Sardar Ajit Singh was an important figure in India's independence movement. He was born in Punjab in

1881 and was the elder brother of the famous revolutionary and martyr, Sardar Bhagat Singh. Sardar Ajit Singh played a significant role in inspiring and mobilizing the youth of Punjab to fight for India's freedom from British colonial rule.

Ajit Singh was educated at Lahore, where he became involved in the Indian National Congress and the freedom struggle. He was particularly inspired by the idea of Swaraj or self-rule, which he believed was essential for the progress and well-being of India's people. He was influenced by the ideas of the extremist leaders, Lala Lajpat Rai and Bal Gangadhar Tilak, and became a leading figure in the revolutionary movement in Punjab.

In 1907, Ajit Singh was arrested and imprisoned for his revolutionary activities. He spent several years in jail, during which time he wrote extensively on political and social issues. After his release, he continued to work for India's freedom and became a prominent leader of the Ghadar Party, a revolutionary organization that aimed to overthrow British rule in India.

Ajit Singh played a key role in organizing the famous 1914 Komagata Maru incident, in which a ship carrying Indian immigrants was denied entry into Canada due to racist immigration policies. The incident galvanized the Indian community and brought attention to the injustice of British colonial rule.

During World War I, Ajit Singh worked closely with the Germans to plan a mutiny of Indian soldiers serving in the British Army. However, the plan was uncovered and Ajit Singh was forced to flee to the United States, where he continued to work for India's freedom.

After returning to India, Ajit Singh played an instrumental role in inspiring and organizing the youth of Punjab to join the freedom struggle. He established a network of revolutionary cells and helped to train and arm young revolutionaries. He also played a key role in the Kakori Train Robbery of 1925, in which a group of revolutionaries stole money from a British train to fund their activities.

Ajit Singh's work for India's freedom continued until his death in 1947, just a few months before India gained independence. His legacy lives on as an inspiration to future generations of Indians to fight for justice and freedom.

In conclusion, Sardar Ajit Singh was a visionary leader who played a key role in inspiring and mobilizing the youth of Punjab to fight for India's freedom. He was a fearless and dedicated revolutionary who spent his life working for the cause of justice and self-rule for India's people. His contributions to the freedom struggle will always be remembered and honored as a crucial part of India's struggle for independence.

5.1.24 Sardar Ujjal Singh

Sardar Ujjal Singh was a prominent figure in the Indian independence movement and served as the

Governor of Punjab after India gained its independence. Born on August 15, 1895, in the town of Naushera in present-day Pakistan, he was one of the leading figures of the Ghadar Party, a revolutionary organization founded by Indian immigrants in the United States and Canada.

As a student in the United States, Sardar Ujjal Singh became involved with the Ghadar Party, which aimed to overthrow British colonial rule in India. He helped to publish the Ghadar newspaper and worked to raise funds and support for the movement. After returning to India, he continued to be involved in revolutionary activities and was imprisoned several times by the British authorities.

During the Quit India Movement in 1942, Sardar Ujjal Singh was arrested and imprisoned for three years.

He was released in 1945 and became a member of the Constituent Assembly of India, which was tasked with drafting the country's constitution. He was also a member of the Indian National Congress and served as a member of the Punjab Legislative Assembly.

After India gained its independence in 1947, Sardar Ujjal Singh played an important role in the integration of the princely states into the newly-formed Indian Union. He was appointed as the Governor of Punjab in 1952 and served in this position until 1957. During his tenure as Governor, he worked to promote the welfare of the people of Punjab and played a key role in the establishment of Punjabi University in Patiala.

Sardar Ujjal Singh was known for his dedication to the cause of Indian independence and his commitment to social justice. He was a strong advocate of communal harmony and worked to bridge the divide between different religious and ethnic communities. He was also a supporter of women's rights and worked to promote gender equality in Indian society.

In recognition of his contributions to the Indian independence movement and his service to the country, Sardar Ujjal Singh was awarded the Padma Bhushan, one of India's highest civilian honors, in 1955. He passed away on February 22, 1983, leaving behind a legacy of service and dedication to the cause of Indian independence and social justice

5.1.25 Sardar Swaran Singh

Sardar Swaran Singh was a prominent leader in the Indian independence movement and a key figure in the post-independence political landscape. He was born on August 19, 1907, in the village of Dulmial in Punjab, British India. He grew up in a family that was actively involved in social and political causes. Sardar Swaran Singh started his political career in the 1920s by joining the Indian National Congress. He was a staunch supporter of the Non-Cooperation Movement and played an active role in organizing protests against the British Raj. He was also a member of the All India Congress Committee and the Punjab Congress Committee.

During the 1940s, Sardar Swaran Singh played a key role in the Indian independence movement. He participated in the Quit India Movement of 1942 and was arrested along with other prominent leaders.

He was imprisoned for three years at the Lahore Fort Jail.

After India gained independence in 1947, Sardar Swaran Singh played an important role in the newly formed government. He served as the Minister of Food and Agriculture from 1947 to 1952 and was instrumental in formulating policies related to food security and agricultural development.

In 1952, Sardar Swaran Singh was elected to the Lok Sabha, the lower house of the Indian parliament. He continued to serve as a member of parliament for the next four decades. During his tenure, he held several important positions, including the Minister of External Affairs from 1964 to 1966 and again from 1970 to 1977.

As the Minister of External Affairs, Sardar Swaran Singh played a key role in shaping India's foreign policy. He was a strong advocate of non-alignment and played an important role in strengthening India's relations with other non-aligned nations. He also played a key role in resolving the Indo-Pakistani War of 1971, which led to the creation of Bangladesh.

Sardar Swaran Singh was known for his honesty, integrity, and commitment to the welfare of the people. He was a respected leader who enjoyed the trust and support of people across party lines. He passed away on May 30, 1994, leaving behind a legacy of service and dedication to the cause of India's freedom and development.

In conclusion, Sardar Swaran Singh's life and career were marked by his unwavering commitment to the cause of Indian independence and his tireless efforts to promote the welfare of the people. He was a respected leader who played an important role in shaping India's political landscape and foreign policy. His legacy continues to inspire and guide the people of India, and his contributions to the nation will always be remembered with gratitude and admiration.

5.1.26 Baba Gurdit Singh

Baba Gurdit Singh was a prominent figure in the Indian independence movement, best known for his role in organizing the Komagata Maru incident, which highlighted the discriminatory policies of the British colonial government towards Indian immigrants. Born on August 1, 1860, in Sarhali, Punjab, Baba Gurdit Singh was a successful businessman and a community leader.

Baba Gurdit Singh became involved in the Indian independence movement in the early 1900s, when he joined the Ghadar Party, a revolutionary organization that aimed to overthrow British rule in India. He provided financial support to the party and also helped to organize the recruitment of Indian soldiers in the British Army who would later rebel against the colonial government.

In 1914, Baba Gurdit Singh became the leader of a group of Indian immigrants who were denied entry into Canada on the Komagata Maru ship, which had sailed from Hong Kong. The ship was carrying 376 passengers, mostly Punjabi Sikhs, who had hopes of starting a new life in Canada. However, the Canadian government, which had recently passed the Continuous Journey regulation, denied them entry on the grounds that they had not made a direct journey from India to Canada. The ship was forced to stay anchored in Vancouver harbor for two months, while the passengers lived in cramped and unsanitary conditions.

Baba Gurdit Singh became the spokesperson for the passengers and fought for their rights to enter Canada. He appealed to the Canadian authorities and the British colonial government to allow the passengers to disembark, but his efforts were unsuccessful. Finally, on July 23, 1914, the Canadian authorities used force to remove the passengers and send them back to India.

The Komagata Maru incident had a profound impact on the Indian independence movement, and Baba

Gurdit Singh's efforts to fight against British colonialism and discrimination inspired many others to join the struggle for independence. His leadership and bravery in the face of adversity became a symbol of the Indian people's determination to fight for their rights and their freedom.

Baba Gurdit Singh continued to be involved in the Indian independence movement until his death on August 17, 1954. He remained committed to the cause of freedom and justice for all people, and his legacy continues to inspire generations of Indians who seek to build a more just and equitable society.

In conclusion, Baba Gurdit Singh's role in the Indian independence movement, particularly his leadership in the Komagata Maru incident, remains a significant part of India's history. His efforts to fight against colonialism and discrimination serve as a reminder of the importance of standing up for one's rights and speaking out against injustice.

5.1.27 Giani Pritam Singh

Giani Pritam Singh was a notable Punjabi freedom fighter and a prominent leader of the Ghadar Party. He played a key role in the Indian independence movement and worked tirelessly to overthrow the British colonial rule in India.

Born on November 21, 1881, in the village of Chabba, in the district of Amritsar, Punjab, Giani Pritam

Singh grew up in a family of farmers. He was educated in traditional Indian schools and later studied at

Khalsa College, Amritsar. It was at college that he became interested in politics and joined the Indian National Congress. He was deeply inspired by the freedom struggle and was influenced by the ideas of Mahatma Gandhi.

In 1913, Giani Pritam Singh left India for the United States and settled in San Francisco. There, he joined the Ghadar Party, a revolutionary organization founded by Punjabi Indians to overthrow British colonial rule in India. Giani Pritam Singh was one of the main organizers of the Ghadar movement in the United States, and he worked closely with other prominent Ghadar leaders, such as Lala Har Dayal and Kartar Singh Sarabha.

In 1914, Giani Pritam Singh returned to India and joined the Ghadar Party's efforts to incite a revolution against the British colonial rule. He played an active role in organizing the party's activities in Punjab and was one of the leaders of the party's first uprising in February 1915. The uprising was suppressed by the British, and many of the leaders, including Giani Pritam Singh, were arrested and imprisoned.

Giani Pritam Singh was released from prison in 1919 and immediately resumed his political activities. He was a vocal critic of the British colonial rule in India and was actively involved in the non-cooperation movement. He also worked to promote social and economic reforms in Punjab and was a strong advocate of women's rights and education.

In 1930, Giani Pritam Singh was arrested again for his involvement in the Salt Satyagraha movement. He was imprisoned for several years and was released in 1934. He continued his political activities and was a prominent leader of the Akali Dal, a political party that aimed to promote Sikh interests.

In 1947, when India gained independence from British colonial rule, Giani Pritam Singh played an active role in the process of the partition of Punjab. He worked to ensure that the interests of the Sikhs were protected in the new political landscape.

Giani Pritam Singh passed away on April 6, 1975, at the age of 93. He is remembered as a courageous freedom fighter who dedicated his life to the cause of Indian independence and the betterment of his people. His legacy continues to inspire generations of Indians to fight for their rights and to work towards a more just and equitable society.

5.1.28 Ajit Kaur

Ajit Kaur was an Indian freedom fighter and social activist who played a significant role in the Indian independence movement. She was born in the village of Begum Pura, Punjab in 1903. Ajit Kaur was raised in a family that valued education and independence, which helped shape her worldview and instilled a strong sense of patriotism in her.

As a young woman, Ajit Kaur joined the Indian National Congress and became involved in various activities related to the freedom movement. She participated in protest marches and organized events to spread awareness about India's struggle for independence. Ajit Kaur also played a crucial role in the Non-Cooperation Movement, which was launched by Mahatma Gandhi in 1920. She led a campaign to boycott British goods and encouraged people to adopt swadeshi (indigenous) products. In 1921, Ajit Kaur participated in the Non-Cooperation Movement's flagship event, the Bardoli Satyagraha, which was a successful campaign against the British-imposed tax on land. She was part of a group of women who traveled to Bardoli to offer their support to the local farmers and workers who were protesting the tax. Ajit Kaur played a significant role in organizing the women's wing of the Satyagraha, which helped mobilize women from all over India to join the movement.

Ajit Kaur's involvement in the freedom movement continued even after India gained independence in 1947. She remained active in social and political work and fought for the rights of women and marginalized communities. In 1950, Ajit Kaur was elected to the Constituent Assembly of India, which was responsible for drafting India's constitution. She played an important role in shaping the country's social and economic policies and advocated for the inclusion of provisions that would benefit women and minorities.

Ajit Kaur's legacy as a freedom fighter and social activist continues to inspire generations of Indians. Her tireless efforts and dedication to the cause of Indian independence helped pave the way for a free and democratic India. Her advocacy for gender and minority rights has also left a lasting impact on Indian society.

5.1.29 Dr. B.R. Nanda

Dr. B.R. Nanda was a historian and a scholar of modern Indian history, known for his works on the Indian National Movement. He was born in Punjab in 1917 and was a witness to the events that led to India's independence in 1947. Nanda's scholarly work on the Indian National Movement and its leaders provided a valuable insight into the socio-political dynamics of the time.

As a historian, Nanda was interested in understanding the historical context of the Indian National Movement and the role played by various leaders in it. In his book "Gandhi and his Critics", he examined the criticisms of Mahatma Gandhi's leadership style and the challenges he faced during the freedom struggle. Nanda also analyzed the evolution of the Congress Party as a mass movement and its role in India's struggle for independence.

One of Nanda's most important contributions to Indian historiography was his work on the Punjab disturbances of 1947. In his book "The Punjab Trilogy", Nanda examined the causes and consequences of the Partition of India and the role played by the leaders of the time in the tragedy. He studied the communal violence that erupted in the region, leading to the displacement of millions of people and the loss of thousands of lives.

Nanda's scholarship was based on meticulous research and a critical examination of historical sources. He believed that a nuanced understanding of history was essential for understanding the complexities of the present. In his writings, he emphasized the importance of studying history from multiple perspectives and the need to recognize the diversity of experiences that shaped the Indian National Movement.

Overall, Dr. B.R. Nanda's contribution to the study of modern Indian history has been invaluable. His works provide a comprehensive understanding of the socio-political context of the Indian National

Movement and the role played by various leaders in it. His research on the Punjab disturbances of 1947 sheds light on one of the most tragic events in Indian history and serves as a reminder of the need to promote communal harmony and understanding

5.1.30 Gurbakhsh Singh Preetlari

Gurbakhsh Singh Preetlari was a renowned Punjabi writer and journalist who played a significant role in the Indian independence movement. Born on 1st March 1916 in the district of Gurdaspur, Punjab, he witnessed the struggles of the Indian people against British colonial rule from a young age. He was an active member of the Communist Party of India and was deeply involved in the struggle for India's independence.

Preetlari was a prolific writer who used his pen to inspire and motivate people to join the independence struggle. He wrote extensively on the social and political issues of his time, and his works had a significant impact on the people of Punjab. His writings were a powerful tool in the fight against colonialism, and he used them to expose the injustices and atrocities committed by the British rulers. Preetlari's involvement in the independence movement was not limited to his writings. He was also an active participant in various political and social movements, including the Quit India Movement of 1942. During this movement, he was arrested and imprisoned for his political activities. However, even in prison, he continued to write and inspire others to fight for their freedom.

After India gained independence in 1947, Preetlari continued his work as a writer and journalist. He wrote about the challenges that India faced after independence, including communalism, poverty, and illiteracy. He also worked tirelessly to promote Punjabi language and culture, and his contributions to Punjabi literature were widely recognized.

Preetlari remained active in politics and was a member of the Communist Party of India until his death in 1960. He was deeply committed to the cause of social justice and remained a strong advocate for the rights of the oppressed and marginalized sections of society.

In conclusion, Gurbakhsh Singh Preetlari was a significant figure in the Indian independence movement. He used his pen and his activism to inspire and motivate people to fight against colonialism and for their freedom. His contributions to Punjabi literature and his commitment to social justice continue to inspire generations of writers and activists.

5.1.31 Udham Singh

Udham Singh, born on 26 December 1899, was a prominent Indian revolutionary and freedom fighter. He is best known for his assassination of Michael O'Dwyer, the former Lieutenant Governor of Punjab, in London in 1940. However, his journey as a revolutionary began much earlier.

Udham Singh was born in a small village in Punjab and was orphaned at a young age. He was brought up in an orphanage in Amritsar, where he became involved in revolutionary activities at a young age. In 1919, when the Jallianwala Bagh massacre took place, Udham Singh was just 20 years old. This incident deeply affected him and inspired him to dedicate his life to the cause of India's independence. Udham Singh became an active member of the Ghadar Party, which was a revolutionary organization that was founded by Punjabi Indians in the United States and Canada in 1913. The party aimed to overthrow British rule in India through armed rebellion. In 1927, Udham Singh was arrested for his involvement in revolutionary activities and was sent to jail in Lahore. He was released in 1931 and went to Europe, where he continued to be involved in revolutionary activities.

On 13 March 1940, Udham Singh assassinated Michael O'Dwyer in London. O'Dwyer was the Lieutenant Governor of Punjab when the Jallianwala Bagh massacre took place, and Udham Singh held him responsible for the incident. After the assassination, Udham Singh was arrested and put on trial. During his trial, he stated that he had acted alone and that he was not a member of any organization. Udham Singh was eventually convicted and sentenced to death. On 31 July 1940, he was hanged at Pentonville Prison in London. His body was then sent back to India, where it was cremated in his hometown of Sunam in Punjab.

Udham Singh's sacrifice and bravery continue to inspire people even today. He is remembered as a hero who dedicated his life to the cause of India's independence and who never wavered in his commitment to the struggle against British rule. His name is inscribed in golden letters in the annals of India's freedom movement, and he will always be remembered as one of the greatest patriots of the country.

5.1.32 Tara Singh Gheba

Tara Singh Gheba was an Indian revolutionary who played a significant role in India's freedom struggle against the British Raj. He was born on 22 February 1895 in Gheba village of Rohtak district in presentday Haryana. Tara Singh Gheba joined the Indian National Congress at an early age and actively participated in the Non-Cooperation Movement led by Mahatma Gandhi. Later, he was drawn towards the revolutionary ideas and became a part of the Hindustan Socialist Republican Association (HSRA), led by Chandra Shekhar Azad and Bhagat Singh.

Tara Singh Gheba's first action with the HSRA was the bombing of the Central Legislative Assembly in

Delhi on 8 April 1929, along with Bhagat Singh and Batukeshwar Dutt. He was later arrested and sentenced to life imprisonment. In the jail, he wrote his autobiography, "Jail Jottings", which became a significant contribution to the revolutionary literature of India.

After his release in 1946, Tara Singh Gheba actively participated in the Quit India Movement and the struggle for Indian independence. He was one of the key organizers of the INA (Indian National Army) in Punjab and was responsible for mobilizing support for the INA among the people. He also played a crucial role in the reorganization of the Communist Party of India (CPI) in Punjab.

Tara Singh Gheba was known for his fearless nature and was revered as a hero among the people. He continued to fight for the rights of the oppressed and exploited even after India gained independence.

He worked for the rights of the farmers and was a strong advocate of the land reform policies.

In 1967, Tara Singh Gheba was elected to the Punjab Legislative Assembly as an independent candidate and later joined the Communist Party of India (Marxist). He passed away on 8 December

1972, leaving behind a legacy of courage, determination, and commitment to the cause of India's freedom and social justice.

In conclusion, Tara Singh Gheba was a freedom fighter, revolutionary, and a social activist who dedicated his life to the cause of India's independence and the betterment of the people. His contribution to the revolutionary literature and his active participation in the Indian freedom struggle will always be remembered as a symbol of courage and patriotism.

5.1.33 Mohan Singh Deb

Mohan Singh Deb was an Indian freedom fighter and a revolutionary who dedicated his life to the cause of India's independence from British rule. Born on 12th October 1899 in Rangamati district in present-day Bangladesh, Deb was deeply influenced by the teachings of Swami Vivekananda and Bhagat Singh, which motivated him to take up the cause of India's freedom.

Deb joined the Indian National Congress in the early 1920s and participated in the Non-Cooperation Movement and the Civil Disobedience Movement, which were led by Mahatma Gandhi. During this period, Deb was arrested and imprisoned several times for his involvement in the freedom struggle. In 1930, Deb became a member of the Hindustan Socialist Republican Association (HSRA), a revolutionary organization that believed in armed struggle against the British. Deb was appointed as the chief organizer of the HSRA in Bengal and played a crucial role in expanding the organization's reach in the region.

In 1931, Deb and his comrades carried out a daring robbery of the Chittagong armory, which was one of the biggest heists of its time. The objective of the robbery was to acquire weapons and ammunition to launch an armed revolution against the British. Although the revolution did not succeed, the Chittagong raid and Deb's role in it became a symbol of resistance against colonial rule.

After the failure of the Chittagong revolution, Deb went underground and continued to work towards India's freedom. He organized revolutionary cells in different parts of India and established contacts with other revolutionary groups, such as the Indian National Army (INA), which was led by Subhas Chandra Bose.

Deb was later arrested by the British authorities in 1934 and was sentenced to life imprisonment. He spent the next 16 years in jail, during which he continued to write and speak out against British rule. He was finally released in 1950, following India's independence.

After his release, Deb became a member of the Communist Party of India and continued to work towards the betterment of the working class. He was elected to the West Bengal Legislative Assembly in 1957 and served as a member of parliament from 1962 to 1967.

Mohan Singh Deb's contributions to India's freedom struggle and his commitment to the ideals of socialism continue to inspire generations of Indians. His life and legacy serve as a reminder of the sacrifices made by countless men and women who fought for India's freedom from colonial rule.

5.1.34 Sardar Vallabhbhai Patel

Sardar Vallabhbhai Patel, popularly known as the "Iron Man of India," was a prominent leader during the Indian independence movement and played a significant role in India's unification after independence.

Born in Gujarat in 1875, Patel was a lawyer by profession and initially practiced in Ahmedabad.

Patel was deeply influenced by Mahatma Gandhi's ideologies and joined the Indian National Congress in

1917. He actively participated in various independence movements, including the Non-Cooperation Movement and the Civil Disobedience Movement. He was imprisoned several times for his involvement in these movements.

One of Patel's most notable contributions to the Indian independence movement was his leadership during the Bardoli Satyagraha in 1928. The British government had imposed high taxes on farmers in the Bardoli region of Gujarat, which led to a widespread protest. Patel emerged as the leader of the movement and led a successful campaign to boycott the taxes. The Bardoli Satyagraha was a significant victory for the Indian independence movement, and Patel's leadership earned him the title of "Sardar," which means leader or chief.

After India gained independence in 1947, Patel played a critical role in integrating the princely states into the newly formed Indian union. He was appointed as the first Deputy Prime Minister of India and the Minister of Home Affairs. Patel was responsible for overseeing the integration of over 550 princely states, and his efforts ensured that the princely states joined the Indian union peacefully.

Patel was also instrumental in establishing the Indian Administrative Service and the Indian Police Service, which are still crucial pillars of India's administrative system. He is widely regarded as the architect of modern India's administrative system.

Unfortunately, Patel's contributions to the Indian independence movement and his role in shaping modern India were largely overshadowed by the more prominent leaders like Mahatma Gandhi and Jawaharlal Nehru. However, in recent years, there has been a renewed interest in Patel's legacy, and he is increasingly being recognized as one of India's greatest leaders.

In conclusion, Sardar Vallabhbhai Patel was a visionary leader who played a vital role in the Indian independence movement and in shaping modern India. His contribution to the integration of princely states and the establishment of India's administrative system is invaluable, and his legacy continues to inspire Indians today.

5.1.35 Shivaram Hari Rajguru

Shivaram Hari Rajguru was one of the three freedom fighters who were hanged by the British authorities for their involvement in the assassination of British police officer, J.P. Saunders, in 1928. Born on August

24, 1908, in a village in Maharashtra, Rajguru was an active member of the Hindustan Socialist

Republican Association (HSRA) and played a significant role in the Indian independence movement. Rajguru's life was heavily influenced by the Jallianwala Bagh massacre of 1919, which he witnessed as a child. This incident left a deep impact on his psyche and fuelled his passion for freedom. He joined the Hindustan Socialist Republican Association (HSRA), which was formed by revolutionaries like

Chandrashekhar Azad, Bhagat Singh and Sukhdev Thapar. Rajguru was actively involved in various revolutionary activities, including the Kakori train robbery in 1925, in which he played a crucial role. The most significant event in Rajguru's life was his involvement in the assassination of J.P. Saunders, a British police officer, in 1928. Along with Bhagat Singh and Sukhdev Thapar, Rajguru planned the killing of Saunders, who was responsible for the brutal lathi charge on Lala Lajpat Rai. On December 17, 1928, they shot Saunders in Lahore and tried to escape. However, they were caught and later hanged on March 23, 1931.

Rajguru's legacy is that of a brave revolutionary who fought for India's freedom. He was deeply committed to the cause of Indian independence and was willing to sacrifice his life for it. His actions and ideology inspired a generation of revolutionaries who played a significant role in India's struggle for independence. Rajguru's name is still remembered with respect and reverence, and he is celebrated as a hero of the Indian independence movement.

In conclusion, Rajguru was a fearless revolutionary who dedicated his life to the cause of Indian independence. He was instrumental in various revolutionary activities and played a significant role in the assassination of J.P. Saunders. Although his life was short, his legacy continues to inspire generations of Indians to fight for justice and freedom. Rajguru will always be remembered as a hero of the Indian independence movement.

5.1.36 Sukhdev Thapar

Sukhdev Thapar was an Indian revolutionary who played a vital role in the Indian independence movement. He was born on May 15, 1907, in Ludhiana, Punjab. He was an active member of the Hindustan Socialist Republican Association (HSRA) and was a close associate of Bhagat Singh and Shivaram Rajguru. Along with them, he was hanged by the British colonial authorities on March 23, 1931, for their involvement in the Lahore conspiracy case. Sukhdev's family was actively involved in India's freedom struggle, and he grew up with a strong sense of patriotism and nationalism. He was an excellent student and graduated from the National College in Lahore. While studying, he met Bhagat Singh and became deeply influenced by his revolutionary ideas. Sukhdev, along with Bhagat Singh and Rajguru, founded the HSRA in 1928, which aimed to overthrow British rule in India through armed struggle. Sukhdev played a crucial role in the HSRA's activities and was involved in several revolutionary activities, including the bombing of the Central Legislative Assembly in Delhi on April 8, 1929. He was also one of the leaders who planned the murder of British police officer J.P. Saunders in Lahore, which eventually led to the Lahore conspiracy case. In the Lahore conspiracy case, Sukhdev, Bhagat Singh, and Rajguru were charged with the murder of Saunders and for planning to wage war against the British government. Despite immense public pressure and widespread protests, the British colonial authorities sentenced them to death by hanging. Sukhdev and his comrades were hanged on March 23, 1931, in Lahore Central Jail. Sukhdev Thapar's sacrifice for the nation became a source of inspiration for many Indians, and he continues to be remembered as a heroic figure in India's independence struggle. His legacy is commemorated through numerous statues and memorials across the country. He is also celebrated on Martyrs' Day, which falls on March 23 every year. Sukhdev's patriotism and unwavering commitment to the cause of

India's freedom have left an indelible mark on the nation's history. His story serves as a reminder of the sacrifices made by countless individuals who fought for India's independence and inspires the younger generation to carry forward the values of freedom, justice, and equality.

5.1.37 Sardar Bahadur Jagat Singh

Sardar Bahadur Jagat Singh was an Indian freedom fighter and political leader who played a significant role in the Indian independence movement. Born on September 23, 1884, in Punjab, Sardar Jagat Singh was a renowned Punjabi leader who worked tirelessly for the betterment of his community. Sardar Jagat Singh joined the Indian National Congress in 1921 and was actively involved in the non-cooperation movement launched by Mahatma Gandhi. He participated in various protests, satyagrahas, and civil disobedience movements, and was imprisoned several times by the British authorities. During the Quit India Movement of 1942, Sardar Jagat Singh played a pivotal role in mobilizing support for the movement in Punjab. He worked closely with other leaders such as

Jawaharlal Nehru, Sardar Patel, and Subhas Chandra Bose to organize the movement and strengthen the Indian National Congress. Sardar Jagat Singh was also a strong advocate of the Punjabi language and culture. He believed that the Punjabi people should have a voice in the Indian independence movement and worked tirelessly to promote Punjabi literature, music, and art. In 1946, Sardar Jagat Singh was elected as the President of the Punjab Provincial Congress Committee, where he worked to strengthen the party's base in Punjab. He played a crucial role in the negotiations that led to the creation of the state of Punjab in 1966, which was a major victory for the Punjabi people. Sardar Jagat Singh's contributions to the Indian independence movement and his advocacy for the Punjabi language and culture have earned him the respect and admiration of people across India. He passed away on February 2, 1966, leaving behind a legacy of courage, commitment, and dedication to the cause of Indian independence. In conclusion, Sardar Bahadur Jagat Singh was a fearless leader who dedicated his life to the struggle for Indian independence and the betterment of the Punjabi people. His contributions to the freedom movement and his tireless advocacy for Punjabi language and culture will always be remembered and celebrated by people across India.

5.1.38 Pandit Harkishan Singh Surjeet

Pandit Harkishan Singh Surjeet was an Indian communist leader who played a prominent role in India's independence movement and later in the country's political landscape. He was born on March 23, 1916,

in the village of Rampur Phul in present-day Punjab, India. Surjeet was an active member of the Communist Party of India (CPI) and served as its General Secretary for more than a decade.

Surjeet's political activism began in his college days, where he joined the All India Students Federation

(AISF), the student wing of the CPI. During this time, he participated in various student protests against British imperialism and advocated for India's independence. After completing his education, he became a full-time political worker and began organizing peasants and workers in the rural areas of Punjab. Surjeet was imprisoned several times for his political activities, including during the Quit India

Movement in 1942. He played a vital role in organizing the peasants' movement in Punjab in the 1950s and 1960s, which advocated for the rights of farmers and laborers. Surjeet was also instrumental in the formation of the Kisan Sabha, a farmers' organization that worked to improve the conditions of farmers in India.

In the 1970s, Surjeet emerged as a prominent leader of the CPI and was elected to the party's Central Committee. He was appointed as the General Secretary of the party in 1992, a position he held until his retirement in 2005. During his tenure as the General Secretary, Surjeet played a crucial role in the formation of the United Front government in 1996, which was supported by a coalition of political parties. The government lasted for two years and implemented several progressive policies, including land reforms and the establishment of the National Commission for Women.

Surjeet was also actively involved in promoting Indo-Pakistani relations and played a critical role in initiating the peace talks between India and Pakistan in the early 2000s. He was a vocal critic of the Bharatiya Janata Party (BJP) and played a crucial role in the formation of the United Progressive Alliance (UPA) government in 2004.

Pandit Harkishan Singh Surjeet was a tireless fighter for social justice and equality, and his contribution to the Indian freedom struggle and the country's political landscape will always be remembered. He passed away on August 1, 2008, at the age of 92, leaving behind a legacy of activism and dedication to the cause of the working class and the oppressed.

In conclusion, Pandit Harkishan Singh Surjeet was an important figure in India's independence movement and a prominent communist leader. His lifelong commitment to the cause of social justice and equality made him a revered figure in the country's political landscape. His contributions to the farmers' and workers' movements in India and his efforts to promote peace and cooperation with Pakistan will always be remembered.

5.1.39 Beant Singh Sandhu

Beant Singh Sandhu was a prominent Sikh revolutionary who played a significant role in India's struggle for independence. Born in the village of Taragarh, Punjab in 1949, Beant Singh was a member of the Khalistan Commando Force, a militant group seeking to establish an independent Sikh state in Punjab. He is best known for his role in the assassination of Indian Prime Minister Indira Gandhi in 1984, which he carried out with Satwant Singh.

Beant Singh's journey towards militancy began with his participation in the Naxalite movement during the 1970s. However, he soon became disillusioned with the movement's focus on class struggle and instead turned his attention to the cause of Sikh separatism. In the late 1970s, he joined the Khalistan Commando Force, which was one of several militant groups operating in Punjab at the time.

The Khalistan Commando Force was formed in 1980 by Manbir Singh Chaheru, a former member of the Indian army. The group's goal was to establish an independent Sikh state called Khalistan, which would encompass Punjab and other areas with a significant Sikh population. The group carried out a number of attacks on Indian security forces and civilians, including the bombing of an Air India flight in 1985 that killed 329 people.

Beant Singh became a key member of the Khalistan Commando Force and was involved in several highprofile attacks. However, his most famous act was the assassination of Indira Gandhi on October 31, 1984. Beant Singh and Satwant Singh were members of Indira Gandhi's security detail, and they used their positions to gain access to her residence. When she emerged from her room, they opened fire on her, killing her on the spot.

Following the assassination, Beant Singh and Satwant Singh were apprehended and put on trial. Both were convicted and sentenced to death. Beant Singh was executed in 1995, while Satwant Singh's sentence was commuted to life imprisonment.

Beant Singh's actions have been a source of controversy in India, with some hailing him as a martyr and others condemning him as a terrorist. His supporters argue that he was fighting for the cause of Sikh self-determination and that his actions were a response to the Indian government's repression of the Sikh community. However, his critics view him as a cold-blooded killer who carried out a senseless act of violence.

Despite the controversy surrounding his actions, there is no doubt that Beant Singh played an important role in India's struggle for independence. His decision to take up arms was a reflection of the deepseated grievances that many Sikhs felt towards the Indian state, and his willingness to put his life on the line for his beliefs has made him a hero to many in the Sikh community

5.1.40 Bhagwan Singh Gyanee

Bhagwan Singh Gyanee was an Indian-American writer, lecturer, and activist who played a significant role in the Indian independence movement. Born on October 5, 1889, in Hoshiarpur, Punjab, he was educated in Punjab and later in the United States, where he obtained a degree in civil engineering. After returning to India, he worked as a journalist, editor, and political activist, joining the Indian National Congress and advocating for Indian independence from British rule.

Gyanee was known for his powerful speeches and writings, which emphasized the importance of India's independence and the need for social and economic justice. He was a staunch supporter of Mahatma Gandhi's non-violent approach to independence and worked closely with other Indian leaders, including Jawaharlal Nehru and Sardar Patel, to achieve India's freedom.

In 1916, Gyanee moved to the United States to pursue further education, obtaining a degree in civil engineering from the University of California, Berkeley. While in the US, he became involved with the Indian independence movement and played a key role in organizing Indian immigrants in the US to support India's independence struggle.

In 1920, Gyanee returned to India and joined the Indian National Congress. He worked as an editor of the Hindustan Times and was an active member of the Congress, participating in several important movements and campaigns, including the Salt Satyagraha and Quit India Movement.

Gyanee also worked tirelessly to promote the cause of Indian independence internationally, traveling to Europe and the United States to speak about the Indian independence movement and to raise funds for the cause. He was also a member of the Indian delegation to the United Nations in 1947 and played a key role in the negotiations that led to India's independence.

In addition to his political activities, Gyanee was a prolific writer and poet. He authored several books, including "The Philosophy of the Bhagavad Gita," which is considered a classic work on Indian philosophy. He also wrote poetry in both English and Punjabi, and his works were widely read and admired.

Throughout his life, Gyanee remained committed to the cause of Indian independence and to the principles of social and economic justice. He was a tireless advocate for the rights of the Indian people and played a significant role in the struggle for India's freedom. His legacy continues to inspire and motivate people around the world today.

5.1.41 Gurdev Singh

Gurdev Singh, also known as Bhai Gurdev Singh, was a prominent figure in the Indian independence movement. He was born on September 21, 1902, in the village of Bagoona, located in present-day Pakistan. He is primarily known for his involvement in the Ghadar Party, a revolutionary organization that sought to overthrow British rule in India.

As a young man, Gurdev Singh was deeply affected by the atrocities committed by the British colonial authorities. He became involved in political activism at a young age, joining the Indian National Congress and later becoming a member of the Ghadar Party.

In 1924, Gurdev Singh was arrested for his revolutionary activities and was sentenced to death. However, his sentence was commuted to life imprisonment, and he was sent to the Cellular Jail in the Andaman and Nicobar Islands. While in prison, he was subjected to inhumane conditions and torture. Despite this, he continued to resist the British colonial authorities and inspire his fellow prisoners.

Gurdev Singh was finally released in 1946, after more than two decades in prison. He returned to his home village of Bagoona, where he continued to work for the cause of Indian independence. He was a vocal critic of the partition of India and worked to ensure that the rights of Sikhs were protected in the newly-formed nations of India and Pakistan.

In the years following India's independence, Gurdev Singh was a respected figure in the political and cultural life of the country. He was an advocate for the rights of farmers and worked to promote Sikh culture and identity.

Gurdev Singh passed away on September 6, 1971, in his home village of Bagoona. He remains a revered figure in the struggle for Indian independence and is remembered for his unwavering commitment to the cause of justice and freedom.

5.1.42 Maulana Habibur RahmanLudhianvi

Maulana Habibur Rahman Ludhianvi was an important figure in the Indian independence movement, known for his advocacy of religious unity and social reform. Born in Ludhiana, Punjab, in 1900, he became a prominent Islamic scholar and was involved in political activism from an early age. As a young man, Ludhianvi joined the Indian National Congress and was deeply influenced by the teachings of Mahatma Gandhi. He was an advocate of non-violent resistance and participated in several civil disobedience campaigns, including the Salt Satyagraha and the Quit India Movement.

Ludhianvi was also a strong proponent of Hindu-Muslim unity and worked tirelessly to promote interfaith harmony. He founded the Punjab Unity Conference in 1935, which aimed to bridge the gap between the two communities and address issues of common concern.

During the partition of India in 1947, Ludhianvi played a critical role in ensuring the safe migration of Hindus and Muslims across the newly created border. He worked closely with other religious leaders to prevent communal violence and promote peace and understanding.

After partition, Ludhianvi remained committed to social reform and continued to speak out against communalism and religious extremism. He was a vocal critic of the Muslim League and the demand for a separate state of Pakistan, arguing that partition would only lead to greater division and conflict. Ludhianvi remained active in politics and served as a member of the Rajya Sabha, the upper house of the Indian parliament, from 1952 to 1958. He was also involved in various social and educational initiatives and established several schools and colleges in Punjab.

Maulana Habibur Rahman Ludhianvi was a tireless advocate for religious unity, social reform, and national independence. His contributions to the Indian independence movement and his efforts to promote interfaith harmony continue to inspire people today.

5.1.43 Ram Singh Kuka

Ram Singh Kuka, also known as Baba Ram Singh, was a prominent leader and reformer who played a significant role in India's struggle for independence. He was born in the early 19th century in Bhaini, a village in Punjab. His early life was marked by poverty, and he grew up witnessing the oppression of the lower castes and the poor. These experiences shaped his worldview, and he became an advocate for social reform and political change.

In the mid-19th century, Ram Singh Kuka founded the Namdhari sect, which aimed to promote a form of Sikhism that emphasized simplicity, equality, and social justice. The sect also challenged the authority of the British colonial rulers and called for the establishment of an independent Indian state. The Namdhari movement gained a significant following, particularly among the lower castes and the rural poor, and it became a thorn in the side of the British authorities.

Ram Singh Kuka's activism and his call for an independent India made him a target of the colonial government. In 1871, he was arrested and charged with sedition. He was sentenced to life imprisonment and sent to the Andaman Islands, where he spent the rest of his life. Despite his imprisonment, the Namdhari movement continued to grow, and it played a significant role in India's struggle for independence.

The Namdhari sect, under the leadership of Ram Singh Kuka's successors, was involved in several important events during the struggle for independence. In 1919, they participated in the Jallianwala Bagh massacre, where hundreds of peaceful protesters were killed by British troops. The Namdharis also played a significant role in the non-cooperation movement and the civil disobedience movement, both of which aimed to challenge British rule in India.

Ram Singh Kuka's legacy continues to inspire generations of activists and reformers in India. His vision of a just and equal society, free from colonial oppression, remains relevant even today. The

Namdhari sect, which he founded, continues to exist and plays an important role in the social, cultural, and political life of Punjab.

In conclusion, Ram Singh Kuka was a visionary leader and social reformer who dedicated his life to the cause of Indian independence. His contributions to the struggle for independence, as well as his advocacy for social justice and equality, have left a lasting impact on Indian society. His story is an inspiration to all those who seek to challenge oppression and work towards a better world.

5.1.44 Sohan Singh Bhakna

Sohan Singh Bhakna was a prominent figure in the Indian independence movement, known for his leadership in organizing peasant movements and advocating for the rights of farmers and laborers. Born in the village of Bhakna in Punjab in 1870, he spent much of his early life working as a laborer on farms and in factories. Inspired by the teachings of Sikhism and the struggle for Indian independence, he became an activist and organizer in the early 20th century.

In 1906, Bhakna played a leading role in founding the Ghadar Party, a revolutionary group of Indian expatriates in the United States that aimed to overthrow British rule in India. He served as the party's president and was responsible for organizing several revolutionary activities, including the publication of the Ghadar newspaper, which advocated for Indian independence and sought to mobilize support among Indian workers abroad.

After returning to India in 1915, Bhakna continued his activism and played a key role in organizing peasant movements in Punjab. He founded the Punjab Kisan Union, which advocated for the rights of farmers and laborers, and led several strikes and protests against British colonial policies. He also worked closely with other independence leaders, including Lala Lajpat Rai and Bhagat Singh, and was imprisoned several times for his political activities.

In 1928, Bhakna played a prominent role in the Bardoli Satyagraha, a successful campaign of civil disobedience against British land revenue policies in Gujarat. He helped organize and lead a group of volunteers who marched to Bardoli to support the movement and provide assistance to the local farmers. The campaign ultimately led to the suspension of the revenue collection and boosted the morale of the Indian independence movement.

Throughout his life, Bhakna remained committed to the cause of Indian independence and the rights of farmers and laborers. He continued to play an active role in politics and social activism until his death in 1968, at the age of 98. His legacy continues to inspire generations of activists and organizers in India and around the world who continue to fight for social justice and equality.

In conclusion, Sohan Singh Bhakna was a dedicated and influential leader in the Indian independence movement, whose advocacy for the rights of farmers and laborers contributed greatly to the struggle for Indian independence. His lifelong commitment to social justice and equality continues to inspire activists and organizers today.

5.1.45 Yashpal

Yashpal (1903-1976) was a renowned Hindi writer, socialist, and freedom fighter who actively participated in the Indian independence movement. Born in Firozpur, Punjab, he was deeply influenced by the nationalist and socialist ideologies and worked tirelessly towards the freedom struggle. Yashpal was actively involved in the Quit India Movement in 1942 and was arrested by the British authorities. During his imprisonment, he wrote his magnum opus, "Jhootha Sach," a novel that exposed the social and economic exploitation of the poor and oppressed in India under British rule. The novel's publication was banned by the British authorities, and its distribution was strictly prohibited. However, it became a popular underground text and contributed significantly to the anti-colonial movement. Yashpal was also involved in the Indian People's Theatre Association (IPTA) and wrote several plays and articles for its magazine. He believed that art and literature should reflect the social realities and problems of the masses and used his writing to raise awareness about issues such as communalism, casteism, and the exploitation of the working class.

After India gained independence in 1947, Yashpal remained active in socialist politics and continued to use his writing as a means of social and political commentary. He wrote several novels, essays, and articles that challenged the dominant narratives of the newly independent India and called for a more equal and just society. His works include "Dhool ke Phool," "Meri Teri Uski Baat," and "Adh Jal Gagari Chhalakat Jaaye."

Yashpal's contribution to the Indian independence movement and his work as a writer and social activist have had a lasting impact on Indian society and literature. He was a recipient of several literary awards, including the Sahitya Akademi Award, and is remembered as a visionary who used his writing to inspire change and promote social justice.

5.1.46 Dharam Singh

Dharam Singh Hayatpur was a pivotal figure in India's struggle for independence. Born in 1893 in the Hayatpur village of Haryana, Dharam Singh grew up in a family that was heavily involved in the Indian independence movement. As a young boy, he was exposed to the ideas of freedom and was deeply influenced by the speeches of leaders like Mahatma Gandhi and Jawaharlal Nehru.

In 1915, Dharam Singh became actively involved in the independence movement and joined the Indian National Congress. He soon became an important member of the party and was known for his strong leadership skills and his ability to inspire people. He was deeply committed to the cause of freedom and worked tirelessly to mobilize people in support of the movement.

Dharam Singh played a key role in several important events during India's struggle for independence. In 1920, he participated in the Non-Cooperation Movement, which was launched by Gandhi to protest against the British rule. Dharam Singh was a prominent leader of the movement in Haryana and led several protests and rallies in the region. He was also instrumental in organizing the Salt Satyagraha in 1930, which was a major turning point in the freedom struggle.

During the Quit India Movement in 1942, Dharam Singh was arrested and imprisoned by the British authorities. However, he continued to work for the cause of freedom even from behind bars. He was released from prison in 1945 and continued to play an active role in the independence movement until India finally achieved independence in 1947.

After independence, Dharam Singh played an important role in the building of the new nation. He was a member of the Constituent Assembly and worked on drafting the Constitution of India. He also served as the Minister of Agriculture and Irrigation in the first government of independent India.

Throughout his life, Dharam Singh remained committed to the ideals of freedom and democracy. He was a true patriot who dedicated his life to the cause of his country. His contributions to India's struggle for independence and his role in building the nation make him a true hero and a source of inspiration for generations to come.

5.1.47 Avtar Singh Pash

Avtar Singh Pash was a revolutionary poet and activist who played a significant role in the Indian independence movement. Born in a small village in Punjab in 1950, Pash grew up in an environment of political turmoil and social upheaval. He was deeply influenced by the socialist and communist ideologies and became involved in political activism at a young age.

In the early 1970s, Pash joined the Naxalite movement, which was a radical left-wing political movement that aimed to overthrow the Indian government through armed struggle. He was arrested and imprisoned several times for his involvement in the movement, but his spirit remained unbroken. In 1978, he was released from prison and continued his activism through his poetry and writings.

Pash was a prolific poet who wrote about a wide range of social and political issues. He was known for his powerful and thought-provoking poems that challenged the status quo and inspired people to fight for their rights. His poetry reflected his deep commitment to the cause of social justice and his unwavering faith in the power of the people to bring about change.

During the 1980s, Pash became increasingly involved in the Sikh separatist movement, which was a movement for the creation of an independent Sikh state in Punjab. However, he soon became disillusioned with the movement and began to criticize its violent methods. He believed that the true path to independence lay in non-violent struggle and the mobilization of the masses.

Tragically, Pash's commitment to the cause of freedom cost him his life. In 1988, he was assassinated by militants who opposed his views. His death was a huge loss to the world of literature and activism, but his legacy lived on. His poems continued to inspire generations of people to fight for their rights and to work towards a just and equitable society.

In conclusion, Avtar Singh Pash was a remarkable individual who devoted his life to the cause of social justice and independence. His unwavering commitment to the cause of freedom, his powerful poetry, and his courageous activism continue to inspire people to this day. His life is a testament to the power of individual courage and the importance of standing up for what one believes in.

5.1.48 Ishar Singh

Ishar Singh was a prominent figure in India's struggle for independence. Born in 1865 in Punjab, he grew up in a family that was deeply committed to the cause of freedom. His father was a freedom fighter who had participated in the Indian Mutiny of 1857.

As a young man, Ishar Singh became involved in the Indian National Congress and began to work towards the cause of independence. He was a prominent leader in the non-cooperation movement of 1920, which was a major campaign against British rule in India. He played a key role in organizing protests and rallies in his home state of Punjab and was known for his fiery speeches and his ability to mobilize people.

During the Salt Satyagraha of 1930, Ishar Singh played a significant role in organizing protests and boycotts against British salt laws. He was arrested and imprisoned for his activism, but his spirit remained unbroken. He continued to work for the cause of independence even while in prison and was released in 1931.

Ishar Singh was deeply committed to the principles of non-violent resistance and believed in the power of peaceful protest to bring about change. He was a close associate of Mahatma Gandhi and worked closely with him on several important campaigns. He was also a staunch advocate for women's rights and played a key role in promoting gender equality.

After India achieved independence in 1947, Ishar Singh continued to work for social justice and equality.

He was a member of the Constituent Assembly and played a key role in drafting the Constitution of India. He also served as a member of parliament and was known for his principled stand on issues of national importance.

In conclusion, Ishar Singh was a true patriot and a tireless fighter for the cause of freedom. His commitment to non-violence and his belief in the power of the people to bring about change continue to inspire generations of Indians. His life is a testament to the importance of standing up for what one believes in and working towards a just and equitable society.

5.1.49 Joginder Singh

Joginder Singh was a courageous fighter for India's independence from British colonial rule. Born in 1902 in Punjab, he grew up in a family that was deeply committed to the cause of freedom. His father was a prominent leader in the Indian National Congress and had been a close associate of Mahatma Gandhi.

In his youth, Joginder Singh was inspired by the non-violent resistance of Gandhi and became actively involved in the Indian independence movement. He participated in numerous protests and rallies, and was often at the forefront of the struggle. He was a passionate speaker and a skilled organizer, and quickly rose to become a prominent leader in his own right.

In 1921, Joginder Singh was arrested for participating in a protest against British rule. He was sentenced to six months in prison, but this did not dampen his spirit. He continued to work for the cause of independence and became increasingly involved in the non-cooperation movement of 1920-1922. In 1930, Joginder Singh participated in the Salt Satyagraha, a major campaign against British salt laws. He was arrested and imprisoned for his activism, but this did not deter him. He continued to work for the cause of freedom even while in prison, and was eventually released in 1931.

Joginder Singh was deeply committed to the principles of non-violence and believed in the power of peaceful protest to bring about change. He was a close associate of Mahatma Gandhi and worked closely with him on several important campaigns. He was also a strong advocate for women's rights and played a key role in promoting gender equality.

After India achieved independence in 1947, Joginder Singh continued to work for social justice and equality. He was a member of the Constituent Assembly and played a key role in drafting the

Constitution of India. He also served as a member of parliament and was known for his principled stand on issues of national importance.

In conclusion, Joginder Singh was a true patriot and a fearless fighter for the cause of freedom. His commitment to non-violence and his belief in the power of the people to bring about change continue to inspire generations of Indians. His life is a testament to the importance of standing up for what one believes in and working towards a just and equitable society.

5.1.50 Sirdar Kapur Singh

Sirdar Kapur Singh was a prominent Sikh intellectual and leader who played a key role in India's struggle for independence from British colonial rule. Born in 1902 in Punjab, he grew up in a family that was deeply involved in Sikh religious and political affairs.

From an early age, Kapur Singh displayed a keen intellect and a strong commitment to social justice. He was a brilliant student and earned a degree in law from the University of Punjab. He was also deeply involved in the Indian independence movement and was a close associate of Mahatma Gandhi.

Kapur Singh was a passionate advocate for the rights of the Sikh community and played a key role in the struggle for Sikh autonomy within the Indian independence movement. He was a vocal critic of British colonialism and of the discriminatory policies of the Indian government towards Sikhs and other minority communities.

In 1946, Kapur Singh was appointed as a member of the Constituent Assembly, which was responsible for drafting India's constitution. He played a key role in shaping the constitutional provisions related to religious freedom and minority rights, and was a staunch defender of the rights of all Indians, regardless of their religion or background.

After India achieved independence in 1947, Kapur Singh continued to work for social justice and equality. He was a member of parliament and served as the governor of Punjab. He also played a key role in the creation of the Shiromani Gurdwara Prabandhak Committee, which was responsible for managing Sikh religious institutions.

Kapur Singh was a prolific writer and intellectual, and his writings continue to be influential in Sikh religious and political circles. He was a fierce defender of Sikh identity and autonomy, and played a key role in shaping the modern Sikh movement.

In conclusion, Sirdar Kapur Singh was a visionary leader and intellectual who made significant contributions to India's struggle for independence and to the cause of social justice and equality. His legacy continues to inspire generations of Sikhs and Indians, and his writings remain an important source of inspiration and guidance for those working towards a just and equitable society.

5.1.51 Lala Hans Raj Gupta

Lala Hans Raj Gupta was a prominent Indian freedom fighter and a close associate of Mahatma Gandhi.

He was born in Rawalpindi, Punjab (now in Pakistan) in 1897, and his family moved to Delhi in 1912. Gupta began his political career as a member of the Indian National Congress, but later joined the Quit India movement and was imprisoned for his participation in it.

Gupta was known for his strong stance against the British colonial government, and he actively participated in various protests and campaigns for India's independence. In 1929, he played a significant role in the Lahore Congress, where the demand for complete independence was raised for the first time. He was also a member of the All India Congress Committee and served as the Chairman of the Delhi Congress Committee.

Gupta was a firm believer in non-violent resistance and actively promoted the idea of Satyagraha, which is the use of nonviolent resistance as a means of social and political change. He played a crucial role in organizing the Salt Satyagraha in Delhi in 1930, which was a significant event in the Indian freedom struggle. The Salt Satyagraha was a nonviolent protest against the British salt tax, which had a significant impact on the Indian economy.

Gupta was a close associate of Mahatma Gandhi and worked closely with him in the Indian National Congress. He was one of the leaders who supported Gandhi during the latter's fast in 1932, which was aimed at achieving better rights for the "untouchables" or Dalits.

In 1942, Gupta participated in the Quit India movement and was arrested by the British colonial authorities. He was imprisoned for three years in Lahore Central Jail, where he was subjected to brutal torture and inhumane conditions. Despite this, he continued to resist the British rule and was a vocal advocate for India's independence.

After India's independence in 1947, Gupta continued to work for social and political reforms in the country. He was a member of the Indian Constituent Assembly and played an active role in drafting the Indian Constitution. He was also a member of the first Lok Sabha, the lower house of the Indian Parliament.

Lala Hans Raj Gupta's contribution to the Indian freedom struggle and his commitment to social and political reforms in independent India make him a prominent figure in Indian history. He passed away in 1968, leaving behind a legacy of courage, dedication, and service to the nation.

5.2 More Contributors

1. Sardul Singh Caveeshar was a prominent Indian socialist and activist who played a key role in the Indian independence movement. He was a vocal critic of British colonialism and worked tirelessly to promote social justice and equality.

2. Shaukat Usmani was an Indian socialist and revolutionary who played a key role in the Indian independence movement. He was a close associate of Bhagat Singh and was involved in several revolutionary activities against British colonial rule.

3. Sundar Singh Majithia was a prominent Indian politician and journalist who played a key role in the Indian independence movement. He was a vocal advocate for Indian independence and worked tirelessly to promote social justice and equality.

4. Waryam Singh Sandhu was an Indian revolutionary and activist who played a key role in the Indian independence movement. He was involved in several revolutionary activities against British colonial rule and was a close associate of Bhagat Singh.

5. Zafar Ali Khan was a prominent Indian journalist and politician who played a key role in the Indian independence movement. He was a vocal advocate for Indian independence and worked tirelessly to promote social justice and equality.

6. Amar Shaheed Baba Deep Singh was a Sikh warrior and martyr who played a key role in the Sikh resistance against Mughal rule in the 18th century. He is remembered for his bravery and sacrifice in defending the Sikh faith and fighting for freedom.

7. Baldev Singh was a prominent Indian politician and revolutionary who played a key role in the Indian independence movement. He was a close associate of Bhagat Singh and was involved in several revolutionary activities against British colonial rule.

8. Chandra Shekhar Azad was an Indian revolutionary and freedom fighter who played a key role in the Indian independence

movement. He was a close associate of Bhagat Singh and was involved in several revolutionary activities against British colonial rule.

9. Darshan Singh Pheruman was an Indian freedom fighter who played a key role in the Indian independence movement. He is remembered for his sacrifice and commitment to the cause of Indian independence, including his involvement in the Quit India Movement.

10. Dhan Singh Bhakhna was a prominent Indian revolutionary and activist who played a key role in the Indian independence movement. He was involved in several revolutionary activities against British colonial rule and was a close associate of Bhagat Singh.

11. Gurmit Singh was a prominent Indian politician and activist who played a key role in the Indian independence movement. He was a vocal advocate for Indian independence and worked tirelessly

to promote social justice and equality.

12. Kartar Singh Duggal was an Indian writer and activist who played a key role in the Indian independence movement. He was a vocal critic of British colonialism and used his writing to raise awareness about the injustices of colonial rule.

13. Narinder Singh Kapoor was an Indian writer and journalist who played a key role in the Indian independence movement. He was a vocal advocate for Indian independence and used his writing to promote social justice and equality.

14. Kartar Singh Jhabbar was an Indian revolutionary and freedom fighter who played a key role in the Indian independence movement. He was involved in several revolutionary activities against British colonial rule and was a close associate of Bhagat Singh.

15. Sardul Singh Caveeshar was a prominent Indian socialist and activist who played a key role in the Indian independence movement. He was a vocal critic of British colonialism and worked tirelessly to promote social justice and equality.

16. Shaukat Usmani was an Indian socialist and revolutionary who played a key role in the Indian independence movement. He was a close

associate of Bhagat Singh and was involved in several revolutionary activities against British colonial rule.

17. Sundar Singh Majithia was a prominent Indian politician and journalist who played a key role in the Indian independence movement. He was a vocal advocate for Indian independence and worked tirelessly to promote social justice and equality.

18. Waryam Singh Sandhu was an Indian revolutionary and activist who played a key role in the Indian independence movement. He was involved in several revolutionary activities against British colonial rule and was a close associate of Bhagat Singh.

19. Zafar Ali Khan was a prominent Indian journalist and politician who played a key role in the Indian independence movement. He was a vocal advocate for Indian independence and worked tirelessly to promote social justice and equality.

20. Prof. Gurbaksh Singh was an Indian scholar and activist who played a key role in the Indian independence movement. He was a vocal advocate for Indian independence and worked tirelessly to promote social justice and equality.

21. Bhai Randhir Singh was a prominent Sikh activist and revolutionary who played a key role in the Indian independence movement. He was involved in several revolutionary activities against British colonial rule and was a close associate of Bhagat Singh. He is remembered for his bravery and sacrifice in defending the Sikh faith and fighting for freedom.

22. Dhanna Singh Gulshan was a prominent Indian socialist and revolutionary who played a key role in the Indian independence movement. He was involved in several revolutionary activities against British colonial rule and was a close associate of Bhagat Singh.

23. Bhai Sahib Singh was a prominent Indian freedom fighter and Sikh activist who played a key role in the Indian independence movement. He was involved in several revolutionary activities against British colonial rule and was a close associate of Bhagat Singh.

24. Raja Mahendra Pratap was an Indian nationalist and revolutionary who played a key role in the Indian independence movement. He was involved in several revolutionary activities against British colonial rule and worked tirelessly to promote social justice and equality.

25. Bhagat Singh Bilga was a prominent Indian revolutionary and socialist who played a key role in the Indian independence movement. He was involved in several revolutionary activities against British colonial rule and was a close associate of Bhagat Singh.

26 . Kanshi Ram was a prominent Indian politician and social activist who played a key role in the Indian independence movement. He worked tirelessly to promote social justice and equality and was a vocal advocate for the rights of marginalized communities.

27. Dr. Amrik Singh was a prominent Indian scholar and activist who played a key role in the Indian independence movement. He was involved in several revolutionary activities against British colonial rule and worked tirelessly to promote social justice and equality.

28. Bhai Jaita was a prominent Sikh activist and revolutionary who played a key role in the Indian independence movement. He was involved in several revolutionary activities against British colonial rule and was a close associate of Guru Gobind Singh.

29. Bhagwati Charan Vohra was an Indian revolutionary and socialist who played a key role in the Indian independence movement. He was involved in several revolutionary activities against British colonial rule and was a close associate of Bhagat Singh.

30. Bhikaiji Cama was a prominent Indian nationalist and revolutionary who played a key role in the Indian independence movement. She was involved in several revolutionary activities against British colonial rule and worked tirelessly to promote social justice and equality.

31. Dalip Singh Saund was a prominent Indian-American politician who played a key role in the Indian independence

movement. He was the first Indian-American to be elected to the US Congress and worked tirelessly to promote social justice and equality for all.

32. Durga Devi Vohra was a prominent Indian feminist and social activist who played a key role in the Indian independence movement. She worked tirelessly to promote women's rights and was a vocal advocate for social justice and equality.

33. Ganga Singh Dhillon was a prominent Indian nationalist and revolutionary who played a key role in the Indian independence movement. He was involved in several revolutionary activities against British colonial rule and worked tirelessly to promote social justice and equality.

34. Giani Pritam Singh Dhillon was a prominent Sikh leader and social activist who played a key role in the Indian independence movement. He worked tirelessly to promote social justice and equality and was a vocal advocate for the rights of marginalized communities.

35. Harnam Singh Tundilat was a prominent Indian socialist and revolutionary who played a key role in the Indian independence movement. He was involved in several revolutionary activities against British colonial rule and was a close associate of Bhagat Singh.

36. Jagat Singh Jagga was a prominent Indian nationalist and revolutionary who played a key role in the Indian independence movement. He was involved in several revolutionary activities against British colonial rule and worked tirelessly to promote social justice and equality.

37. Jathedar Santokh Singh was a prominent Sikh leader and social activist who played a key role in the Indian independence movement. He worked tirelessly to promote social justice and equality and was a vocal advocate for the rights of marginalized communities.

38. Kartar Singh Virk was a prominent Indian socialist and revolutionary who played a key role in the Indian independence movement. He was involved in several revolutionary activities against

British colonial rule and worked tirelessly to promote social justice and equality.

39. Khushwant Singh was a prominent Indian author and journalist who played a key role in the Indian independence movement. He worked tirelessly to promote social justice and equality and was a vocal advocate for the rights of marginalized communities.

40. Nanak Singh was a prominent Indian novelist and social activist who played a key role in the Indian independence movement. He worked tirelessly to promote social justice and equality and was a vocal advocate for the rights of marginalized communities.

41. Pal Singh Purewal was a prominent Indian scholar and inventor who played a key role in the Indian independence movement. He is most famous for creating the Nanakshahi calendar, a Sikh calendar that is widely used throughout the world today.

42. Pritam Singh Dhillon was a prominent Indian revolutionary and nationalist who played a key role in the Indian independence movement. He was involved in several revolutionary activities against British colonial rule and was a close associate of Bhagat Singh.

43. Raja Aziz Bhatti was a prominent Pakistani military officer who played a key role in the IndoPakistani War of 1965. He was posthumously awarded the Nishan-e-Haider, Pakistan's highest military award, for his bravery and sacrifice during the war.

44. Raja Lachhman Singh was a prominent Indian nationalist and revolutionary who played a key role in the Indian independence movement. He was involved in several revolutionary activities against British colonial rule and worked tirelessly to promote social justice and equality.

45. Ram Saran Das was a prominent Indian socialist and revolutionary who played a key role in the Indian independence movement. He was involved in several revolutionary activities against British colonial rule and worked tirelessly to promote social justice and equality.

46 . Santokh Singh Kalra, better known by his pen name "Punjabi", was a prominent Indian author and journalist who played a key role in the Indian independence movement. He worked tirelessly to promote social justice and equality and was a vocal advocate for the rights of marginalized communities.

47. Sardar Dyal Singh Majithia was a prominent Indian philanthropist and entrepreneur who played a key role in the Indian independence movement. He founded several institutions, including The Tribune newspaper, to promote education and social justice.

48 . Sardar Kesar Singh Tikka was a prominent Indian nationalist and revolutionary who played a key role in the Indian independence movement. He was involved in several revolutionary activities against British colonial rule and worked tirelessly to promote social justice and equality.

49. Sardar Nand Singh was a prominent Indian nationalist and revolutionary who played a key role in the Indian independence movement. He was involved in several revolutionary activities against British colonial rule and worked tirelessly to promote social justice and equality.

50. Sardar Singh Ragi was a prominent Indian musician and social activist who played a key role in the Indian independence movement. He used his music to promote social justice and equality and was a vocal advocate for the rights of marginalized communities.

51. Satguru Jagjit Singh was a spiritual leader who played an important role in the Indian independence movement. He led the Namdhari sect and was actively involved in civil disobedience movements. He believed in the power of non-violence and was a strong advocate of communal harmony. Satguru Jagjit Singh was also instrumental in organizing the Quit India Movement in Punjab.

52. Sohan Singh Bhakna was a labor leader and one of the founding members of the Ghadar Party. He played a crucial role in organizing the Indian diaspora in North America to support the Indian

independence movement. Bhakna was arrested multiple times by the British authorities and spent several years in prison for his activism.

53. Sujan Singh Uban was a freedom fighter and member of the Indian National Congress. He participated in the Salt Satyagraha and was arrested by the British authorities. Uban was also a member of the Punjab Legislative Council and worked towards the development of the region.

54. Sunder Singh Lyallpuri was a politician and social activist who played a key role in the Indian independence movement. He was a member of the Indian National Congress and served as the president of the Punjab Pradesh Congress Committee. Lyallpuri participated in various civil disobedience movements and was imprisoned several times by the British authorities.

55. Swaran Singh Kahlon was a political leader and member of the Communist Party of India. He was a vocal advocate of workers' rights and played an important role in the labor movement. Kahlon was also actively involved in the Indian independence movement and was imprisoned by the British authorities for his activism.

56. Teja Singh Samundri was a Sikh leader and member of the Indian National Congress. He participated in various non-violent protests and was a strong advocate of communal harmony. Samundri was also a member of the Punjab Legislative Council and worked towards the upliftment of the Sikh community.

57. Ujagar Singh was a revolutionary and member of the Ghadar Party. He participated in the Ghadar Conspiracy, a plan to overthrow British rule in India. Singh was arrested and sentenced to death for his role in the conspiracy.

58 . Veer Savarkar was a prominent leader of the Indian independence movement and a founding member of the Hindu nationalist organization, Rashtriya Swayamsevak Sangh (RSS). He was also a member of the Hindu Mahasabha and advocated for the

establishment of a Hindu Rashtra. Savarkar was imprisoned by the British authorities for his role in the revolutionary activities.

59. Virendranath Chattopadhyaya, also known as Chatto, was a revolutionary and member of the Ghadar Party. He played a crucial role in organizing the Indian diaspora in North America and worked towards overthrowing British rule in India. Chattopadhyaya was arrested and imprisoned multiple times by the British authorities.

60. Zora Singh Sohi was a freedom fighter and member of the Indian National Congress. He participated in various non-violent protests and was imprisoned by the British authorities for his activism. Sohi also worked towards the development of the region and was a member of the Punjab Legislative Assembly.

61. Saroop Singh Kadian was an Indian revolutionary who participated in the Indian independence movement. He was a member of the Ghadar Party and was involved in organizing and leading antiBritish activities. He was arrested and sentenced to life imprisonment for his involvement in the Lahore Conspiracy Case. He was released from prison in 1945.

62. Bhagwati Charan was an Indian revolutionary who played a key role in the Kakori Conspiracy of 1925. He was a member of the Hindustan Socialist Republican Association (HSRA) and was involved in several acts of sabotage against the British. He was arrested and sentenced to death in the Lahore Conspiracy Case. He died in prison in 1931.

63. Baldev Singh was an Indian revolutionary who was a member of the Ghadar Party. He participated in several anti-British activities and was arrested and sentenced to life imprisonment for his involvement in the Lahore Conspiracy Case. He was released from prison in 1945.

64. Bawa Harkishan Singh was an Indian freedom fighter and a member of the Ghadar Party. He was actively involved in organizing and leading anti-British activities in Punjab and was arrested and

sentenced to death in the Lahore Conspiracy Case. His sentence was commuted to life imprisonment, and he was released from prison in 1945.

65. Bhag Singh Ankhi was an Indian revolutionary who was a member of the Ghadar Party. He was actively involved in organizing and leading anti-British activities and was arrested and sentenced to life imprisonment for his involvement in the Lahore Conspiracy Case. He was released from prison in 1945.

66. Bhagwan Singh was an Indian revolutionary who was a member of the Ghadar Party. He was actively involved in organizing and leading anti-British activities and was arrested and sentenced to life imprisonment for his involvement in the Lahore Conspiracy Case. He was released from prison in 1945.

67. Bhai Parmanand was an Indian freedom fighter who was involved in the Indian independence movement. He was a member of the Indian National Congress and was actively involved in organizing and leading anti-British activities. He was arrested several times for his involvement in the movement.

68. Bishen Singh Bedi was an Indian cricketer and a left-arm spinner who played for the Indian cricket team from 1966 to 1979. He was known for his accuracy and flight in his bowling and was a part of India's famous spin quartet in the 1970s.

69. Chaudhary Rehmat Ali was a Pakistani nationalist who is best known for coining the term "Pakistan" in 1933. He was a strong advocate for the creation of a separate Muslim state in South Asia and is considered to be one of the founders of Pakistan.

70. Dalip Singh Pandhi was an Indian revolutionary who was a member of the Ghadar Party. He was actively involved in organizing and leading anti-British activities and was arrested and sentenced to life imprisonment for his involvement in the Lahore Conspiracy Case. He was released from prison in 1945.

71. Dr. Kartar Singh Garewal was an Indian freedom fighter who was involved in the Indian independence movement. He was a member of the Indian National Congress and was actively involved in organizing and leading anti-British activities. He was arrested several times for his involvement in the movement.

72. Fateh Singh Pandor was an Indian revolutionary who was a member of the Ghadar Party. He was actively involved in organizing and leading anti-British activities and was arrested and sentenced to life imprisonment for his involvement in the Lahore Conspiracy Case. He was released from prison in 1945.

73. Giani Gurmukh Singh Musafir was a prominent Sikh scholar and religious leader who played an active role in the Indian independence movement. He was a close associate of Mahatma Gandhi and supported the nonviolent civil disobedience movement. He was also a strong advocate for the rights of Sikhs and worked to promote their cultural and religious heritage.

74. Giani Sant Singh Maskeen was a renowned Sikh scholar and theologian who was deeply committed to the cause of Indian independence. He was a staunch supporter of nonviolence and worked tirelessly to promote the teachings of Guru Nanak and other Sikh saints. He also played an active role in promoting interfaith harmony and understanding.

75. Gurbax Singh Preetlari was a revolutionary poet and writer who played an important role in the Indian independence movement. He used his pen to spread the message of freedom and justice and was an influential figure in the Punjabi literary world. His poetry and writings inspired many people to join the struggle for independence.

76 . Hardit Singh Malik was the first Indian pilot to serve in the Royal Flying Corps during World War I. He later became a diplomat and played an important role in the Indian independence movement. He was a close associate of Mahatma Gandhi and worked to promote Indian interests on the international stage.

77. Inderjit Singh Reyat was a Canadian Sikh who was involved in the 1985 bombing of Air India Flight 182. The bombing, which killed 329 people, was one of the deadliest acts of terrorism in Canadian history. Reyat was eventually convicted and sentenced to prison for his role in the attack.

78 . Jagjit Singh Chauhan was a Sikh nationalist who was involved in the movement for Khalistan, an independent Sikh state in India. He was the founder of the Khalistan movement and worked to promote Sikh interests in India and abroad. He was eventually forced to flee India and spent the rest of his life in exile.

79. Jaspal Bhatti was a popular Indian comedian and satirist who used humor to critique the social and political issues of his time. He was known for his sharp wit and biting satire, and his work played an important role in raising awareness about corruption and injustice in Indian society.

80. Joginder Singh Puar was an Indian freedom fighter who played an active role in the struggle for independence. He was a member of the Indian National Army, which was formed to fight against British rule in India. He was eventually captured and sentenced to prison, but his sacrifice and bravery inspired many others to join the independence movement.

81. Jwala Singh was a Sikh revolutionary who led the Babbar Akali movement, which aimed to overthrow British rule in India. He was known for his daring raids on British targets and was eventually captured and sentenced to death.

82. Khushwant Singh was a prominent Indian writer and journalist who played an active role in the Indian independence movement. He was a close associate of Mahatma Gandhi and worked as a journalist for several Indian newspapers. He also served as a member of Parliament and was a strong advocate for secularism and democracy.

83. Kiranjit Kaur was a freedom fighter who was active in the Indian independence movement. She was a member of the Indian

National Army and played an important role in the Azad Hind Fauj, which fought against British rule in India.

84. Mahashay Rajpal was a publisher who was known for his nationalist views and support for the Indian independence movement. He published several books and magazines that promoted the cause of Indian freedom, including "Veer Bharat" and "Kranti."

85. Mohinder Singh Pujji was an Indian soldier who fought in World War II and later joined the Indian independence movement. He was a member of the Indian National Army and fought against the British in Burma and other parts of Southeast Asia.

86. Nand Singh Grewal was a prominent Indian revolutionary who was active in the Ghadar movement, which aimed to overthrow British rule in India. He was known for his fiery speeches and was a close associate of other revolutionary leaders, including Bhagat Singh and Chandrashekhar Azad.

87. Prithipal Singh was an Indian field hockey player who represented India at the 1948 and 1952 Olympic Games. He was also a member of the Indian independence movement and was known for his support of nonviolent resistance and civil disobedience.

88. Puran Singh was a Sikh scholar and poet who was deeply committed to the cause of Indian independence. He wrote extensively on Sikh spirituality and also supported the nonviolent civil disobedience movement led by Mahatma Gandhi.

89. Raghubir Singh Sandhu was a prominent Indian revolutionary who was active in the Ghadar movement. He was known for his courage and bravery and played an important role in several key revolutionary activities, including the Lahore conspiracy case.

90. Randhir Singh was a prominent Indian revolutionary who was active in the Indian National Army. He fought against the British in Burma and other parts of Southeast Asia and was a close associate of other Indian nationalist leaders, including Subhas Chandra Bose.

91. Ram Chander was an Indian revolutionary who was active in the Indian independence movement. He was a member of the Hindustan Socialist Republican Association and played an important role in several key revolutionary activities, including the Kakori train robbery.

92. Ram Singh Kuka was a Sikh religious leader and social reformer who played an important role in the Indian independence movement. He founded the Kuka movement, which aimed to promote social and economic equality among different castes and religions in India.

93. Sham Singh Attariwala was an Indian revolutionary who was active in the Ghadar movement. He played an important role in several key revolutionary activities, including the attack on the Malerkotla police station and the mutiny of the 5th Light Infantry in Singapore.

94. Shyamji Krishnavarma was an Indian revolutionary who was active in the Indian independence movement. He founded the Indian Home Rule Society in London and played an important role in mobilizing support for the cause of Indian freedom among the Indian diaspora in Britain and other parts of Europe.

95. Sukhdev Singh Babbar was an Indian revolutionary who was active in the Babbar Akali movement. He was known for his daring raids on British targets and was eventually captured and executed along with other prominent Babbar Akali leaders, including Bhagat Singh and Rajguru.

96 . Suniti Chaudhary was an Indian revolutionary who was active in the Indian National Army. She played an important role in the INA's women's wing and was also involved in several key revolutionary activities, including the Burma campaign.

97. Tara Singh Narottam was an Indian revolutionary who was active in the Hindustan Socialist Republican Association. He played

an important role in several key revolutionary activities, including the Kakori train robbery and the Lahore conspiracy case.

98 . Zia Ul Haq was a Pakistani military ruler who played an important role in the geopolitics of South Asia in the 1980s. He was known for his support of Islamist extremism and played a key role in the Soviet-Afghan War.

99. Ajoy Ghosh was an Indian communist leader who played an important role in the Indian independence movement. He was a member of the Communist Party of India and was a strong advocate for socialist principles and the rights of workers and peasants in India.

100. Arur Singh was an Indian revolutionary who was active in the Indian independence movement. He was a member of the Hindustan Socialist Republican Association and played an important role in several key revolutionary activities, including the Kakori train robbery and the Lahore conspiracy case.

101. Atma Singh was an Indian revolutionary who was active in the Indian independence movement. He was a member of the Ghadar Party and played an important role in several key revolutionary activities, including the attack on the Mian Mir Cantonment in Lahore.

102. Baba Gurdit Singh was a Punjabi Indian Sikh who played an important role in the Ghadar movement. He organized the Komagata Maru incident, in which a group of Indian passengers aboard a Japanese steamship were denied entry into Canada due to racist immigration laws.

103. Baba Khem Singh Bedi was an Indian revolutionary who was active in the Indian independence movement. He was a member of the Ghadar Party and played an important role in several key revolutionary activities, including the assassination of Sir Michael O'Dwyer.

104. Baba Nidhan Singh Chugha was an Indian revolutionary who was active in the Indian independence movement. He was a member of the Ghadar Party and played an important role in several key

revolutionary activities, including the attack on the Mian Mir Cantonment in Lahore.

105. Baba Ram Singh Namdhari was an Indian religious leader and social reformer who played an important role in the Indian independence movement. He founded the Namdhari sect and was known for his opposition to British rule and his efforts to promote social and economic equality in India.

106. Baba Thakur Singh was an Indian Sikh religious leader who played an important role in the

Khalistan movement. He was the head of the Damdami Taksal, a Sikh seminary, and was known for his strong advocacy of Sikh nationalism and his opposition to Indian rule.

107. Bal Mukund was an Indian revolutionary who was active in the Indian independence movement. He was a member of the Hindustan Socialist Republican Association and played an important role in several key revolutionary activities, including the Kakori train robbery and the Lahore conspiracy case.

108 . Baldev Singh Khera was an Indian revolutionary who was active in the Indian independence movement. He was a member of the Hindustan Socialist Republican Association and played an important role in several key revolutionary activities, including the Kakori train robbery and the Lahore conspiracy case.

109. Balraj Sahni was an Indian film actor and writer who was known for his strong social and political activism. He was an outspoken critic of British colonialism and played an important role in the Indian independence movement.

110. Banta Singh was an Indian revolutionary who was active in the Indian independence movement. He was a member of the Hindustan Socialist Republican Association and played an important role in several key revolutionary activities, including the Kakori train robbery and the Lahore conspiracy case.

111. Bawa Harkishan Singh was an Indian spiritual leader and social activist who was active in the Indian independence movement. He founded the Sant Nirankari Mission, a spiritual organization that promoted social and religious unity and worked towards eradicating social evils like untouchability.

112. Bhagwan Singh Gyanee was an Indian revolutionary who was active in the Indian independence movement. He was a member of the Ghadar Party and played an important role in several key revolutionary activities, including the Lahore conspiracy case.

113. Bhagwan Singh Sohan Singh was an Indian revolutionary who was active in the Indian independence movement. He was a member of the Ghadar Party and played an important role in several key revolutionary activities, including the attack on the Mian Mir Cantonment in Lahore.

114. Bhim Sen Sachar was an Indian politician and social activist who was active in the Indian independence movement. He was a prominent member of the Indian National Congress and played an important role in the freedom struggle.

115. Bhola Paswan Shastri was an Indian politician and social activist who was active in the Indian independence movement. He was a prominent member of the Indian National Congress and played an important role in the freedom struggle.

116 . Bishan Singh Bedi was an Indian cricketer who played for the Indian national team. He was known for his left-arm spin bowling and was also involved in social activism, including supporting the Dalit rights movement.

117. Bishen Singh Sahni was an Indian author and playwright who was known for his works that explored social and political issues. He was involved in the Indian independence movement and was an active member of the Indian National Congress.

118 . Chaman Lal Chaman was an Indian poet and writer who was known for his contributions to the Hindi literature. He was also

involved in social activism and was a member of the Indian National Congress.

119. Chandra Shekhar Azad was an Indian revolutionary who was active in the Indian independence movement. He was a member of the Hindustan Socialist Republican Association and played an important role in several key revolutionary activities, including the Kakori train robbery and the Lahore conspiracy case.

120. Chetan Anand was an Indian film director, producer and screenwriter who was known for his films that explored social and political issues. He was involved in the Indian independence movement and was an active member of the Indian National Congress.

121. Darbara Singh Guru was an Indian politician and social activist who was active in the Indian independence movement. He was a prominent member of the Indian National Congress and played an important role in the freedom struggle.

122. Daulat Ram Gupta was an Indian politician and social activist who was active in the Indian independence movement. He was a prominent member of the Indian National Congress and played an important role in the freedom struggle.

123. Dhan Gopal Mukerji was an Indian writer and lecturer who was known for his works that explored the Indian culture and society. He was involved in the Indian independence movement and was an active member of the Indian National Congress.

124. Dharam Singh Hayatpur was an Indian politician and social activist who was active in the Indian independence movement. He was a prominent member of the Indian National Congress and played an important role in the freedom struggle.

125. Dhian Singh was an Indian revolutionary who was active in the Indian independence movement. He was a member of the Ghadar Party and played an important role in several key revolutionary activities.

126. Diwan Chaman Lall was an Indian politician and social activist who was active in the Indian independence movement. He was a prominent member of the Indian National Congress and played an important role in the freedom struggle.

127. Dr. M.S. Randhawa was an Indian civil servant and social activist who was active in the Indian independence movement. He was a prominent member of the Indian National Congress and played an important role in the freedom struggle.

128 . G.S. Dhillon was an Indian politician and social activist who was active in the Indian independence movement. He was a prominent member of the Indian National Congress and played an important role in the freedom struggle.

129. Gauri Shankar Gupta was an Indian politician and social activist who was active in the Indian independence movement. He was a prominent member of the Indian National Congress and played an important role in the freedom struggle.

130. Gian Singh Rarewala was an Indian politician and social activist who was active in the Indian independence movement. He was a prominent member of the Indian National Congress and played an important role in the freedom struggle.

131. Giani Kartar Singh was an Indian politician and social activist who was active in the Indian independence movement. He was a prominent member of the Indian National Congress and played an important role in the freedom struggle.

132. Giani Sant Singh Maskeen was an Indian writer and scholar who was known for his works on Sikhism and the Indian culture. He was involved in the Indian independence movement and was an active member of the Indian National Congress.

133. Giani Sher Singh Ambala was an Indian writer and scholar who was known for his works on Sikhism and the Indian culture. He was involved in the Indian independence movement and was an active member of the Indian National Congress.

134. Gopal Singh Nepali was an Indian poet and writer who was known for his works on the Indian culture and society. He was involved in the Indian independence movement and was an active member of the Indian National Congress.

135. Gurdial Singh Dhillon was an Indian politician and social activist who was active in the Indian independence movement. He was a prominent member of the Indian National Congress and played an important role in the freedom struggle.

136. Gurmeet Kanwal was an Indian writer and social activist who was active in the Indian independence movement. He was a prominent member of the Indian National Congress and played an important role in the freedom struggle.

137. Har Dayal was an Indian revolutionary and social activist who was active in the Indian independence movement. He was a member of the Ghadar Party and played an important role in several key revolutionary activities.

138. Harnam Singh Saini was an Indian politician and social activist who was active in the Indian independence movement. He was a prominent member of the Indian National Congress and played an important role in the freedom struggle.

139. Hazari Lal was an Indian politician and social activist who was active in the Indian independence movement. He was a prominent member of the Indian National Congress and played an important role in the freedom struggle.

140. Inder Kumar Gujral was an Indian politician and statesman who served as the Prime Minister of India from 1997 to 1998. He was involved in the Indian independence movement and was an active member of the Indian National Congress.

141. Jagjit Singh Chauhan: Jagjit Singh Chauhan was a pro-Khalistan activist who played a significant role in the Sikh separatist movement. He founded the Khalistan movement and was known for advocating an independent Sikh state in India. Chauhan

was also associated with various militant groups, including the Babbar Khalsa International, and was arrested multiple times for his involvement in terrorist activities.

142. Jasbir Singh Athwal: Jasbir Singh Athwal was a British Indian who played a crucial role in the Indian independence movement. He was a member of the Ghadar Party and was actively involved in planning and executing revolutionary activities against the British Raj. He was arrested in 1914 and sent to the Andaman Islands, where he spent several years in prison.

143. Jasbir Singh Bains: Jasbir Singh Bains was an Indian freedom fighter who participated in the Quit India Movement and was also a member of the Indian National Army. He was involved in several nationalist activities and played a significant role in the Indian independence movement. After India gained independence, Bains served as a Member of Parliament and was also appointed as the governor of Pondicherry.

144. Jassa Singh Ahluwalia: Jassa Singh Ahluwalia was a prominent Sikh leader who played a crucial role in the Sikh Empire's formation in the 18th century. He was one of the founding members of the Khalsa, a military force created by Guru Gobind Singh to fight against the Mughal Empire.

Ahluwalia played a significant role in various battles and was known for his bravery and military skills.

145. Karam Singh: Karam Singh was an Indian freedom fighter who participated in the Indian independence movement. He was a member of the Indian National Congress and was actively involved in various nationalist activities. Karam Singh was also a member of the Punjab Legislative Assembly and served as the Minister of Agriculture and Irrigation in the Punjab government.

146 . Karam Singh Mann: Karam Singh Mann was an Indian freedom fighter who played a crucial role in the Indian independence movement. He was a member of the Ghadar Party and was actively

involved in revolutionary activities against the British Raj. Mann was arrested in 1914 and sent to the Andaman Islands, where he spent several years in prison.

147. Kesar Singh Narula: Kesar Singh Narula was an Indian freedom fighter who participated in the Indian independence movement. He was a member of the Indian National Congress and was actively involved in various nationalist activities. Narula was also a member of the Punjab Legislative Assembly and served as the Minister of Food and Civil Supplies in the Punjab government.

148. Khushwant Singh: Khushwant Singh was an Indian writer and journalist who played a significant role in shaping the Indian literary and political landscape. He was associated with various newspapers and magazines, including The Illustrated Weekly of India, The Hindustan Times, and The National Herald. Singh was also a member of the Rajya Sabha and was awarded the Padma Bhushan in 1974.

149. Kirpal Singh: Kirpal Singh was an Indian freedom fighter who participated in the Indian independence movement. He was a member of the Indian National Congress and was actively involved in various nationalist activities. Singh was also a member of the Punjab Legislative Assembly and served as the Minister of Public Works in the Punjab government.

150. Kishan Singh Gargaj: Kishan Singh Gargaj was an Indian freedom fighter who played a crucial role in the Indian independence movement. He was associated with various revolutionary groups, including the Hindustan Socialist Republican Association and the Kirti Kisan Party. Gargaj was actively involved in planning and executing revolutionary activities against the British Raj and was arrested multiple times for his involvement in nationalist activities.

151. Manohar Singh Gill: Manohar Singh Gill was an Indian police officer who played a significant role in suppressing the Khalistan movement during the 1980s and 1990s. He was appointed as the

Director General of Police (DGP) of Punjab in 1991 and was instrumental in carrying out the Operation Black Thunder to flush out militants from the Golden Temple in 1988. He was known for his controversial methods and has been both criticized and praised for his actions during his tenure as DGP.

152. Mohan Singh Josan: Mohan Singh Josan was an Indian freedom fighter and political leader who actively participated in the Indian independence movement. He was a member of the Ghadar Party, a revolutionary organization that aimed to overthrow British rule in India. He was also a founding member of the All India Kisan Sabha and played a key role in the farmers' movements in Punjab.

153. Narain Singh: Narain Singh was an Indian politician and a prominent leader of the Akali Dal party.

He was elected to the Punjab Legislative Assembly several times and served as a minister in the Punjab government. He was a strong advocate of the rights of the Sikh community and played an important role in the Akali Dal's campaign for a separate state of Punjab.

154. Narain Singh Chaura: Narain Singh Chaura was an Indian revolutionary and a member of the Ghadar Party. He was involved in several revolutionary activities against British rule in India, including the Lahore conspiracy case of 1915. He was later imprisoned in the Andaman and Nicobar Islands for his involvement in the Indian independence movement.

155. Pannalal Ghosh: Pannalal Ghosh was an Indian classical flautist and one of the pioneers of the Hindustani classical music tradition. He is credited with popularizing the Bansuri, a bamboo flute, and has made significant contributions to Indian classical music. He was awarded the Padma Bhushan, one of India's highest civilian honors, in 1970.

156. Parkash Singh Badal: Parkash Singh Badal is an Indian politician and a prominent leader of the Shiromani Akali Dal party. He has served as the Chief Minister of Punjab five times and has been a

member of the Punjab Legislative Assembly for several terms. He has played a key role in the politics of Punjab and has been instrumental in the Akali Dal's campaign for a separate state of Punjab.

157. Piara Singh Gill: Piara Singh Gill was an Indian physicist who made significant contributions to the field of nuclear physics. He was a professor at the University of California, Los Angeles and was awarded the Padma Shri, one of India's highest civilian honors, in 1988. He was also a member of the Royal Society of London and a Fellow of the American Physical Society.

158. Pritam Singh Daulta: Pritam Singh Daulta was an Indian revolutionary and a member of the Ghadar

Party. He was involved in several revolutionary activities against British rule in India, including the Lahore conspiracy case of 1915. He was later imprisoned in the Andaman and Nicobar Islands for his involvement in the Indian independence movement.

159. Rajendra Prasad: Rajendra Prasad was an Indian politician and the first President of India. He played a key role in the Indian independence movement and was a close associate of Mahatma Gandhi. He was also a prominent leader of the Indian National Congress and served as the

President of the party several times. He is remembered as one of India's greatest statesmen.

160. Ram Singh Thakur: Ram Singh Thakur was an Indian revolutionary and a member of the Hindustan Socialist Republican Association. He was involved in several revolutionary activities against British.

161. Sahib Singh Sokhey: Sahib Singh Sokhey was an Indian freedom fighter who actively participated in the Indian independence movement. He was a member of the Hindustan Socialist Republican Association (HSRA) and was involved in the Kakori conspiracy of 1925. He also played a key role in the Lahore conspiracy case of 1930

and was sentenced to life imprisonment. After India's independence, he served as a member of the Rajya Sabha.

162. Sardar Bahadur Jagat Singh: Sardar Bahadur Jagat Singh was an Indian freedom fighter and a member of the Indian National Congress. He played a significant role in the Quit India Movement and was imprisoned by the British for his participation. After India's independence, he served as a member of the Lok Sabha and the Rajya Sabha.

163. Sardar Bahadur Sir Bhupindra Singh: Sardar Bahadur Sir Bhupindra Singh was the ruling Maharaja of the princely state of Patiala from 1900 to 1938. He actively supported the Indian independence movement and was a member of the All India Congress Committee. He was also a signatory to the Lahore resolution of 1929. After India's independence, he served as the Rajpramukh of the newly created state of PEPSU.

164. Sardul Singh Caveeshar: Sardul Singh Caveeshar was an Indian revolutionary and a member of the Hindustan Socialist Republican Association (HSRA). He was involved in several revolutionary activities, including the Kakori conspiracy of 1925 and the Lahore conspiracy case of 1930. He was arrested and imprisoned by the British for his participation in the independence movement.

165. Shiv Kumar Batalvi: Shiv Kumar Batalvi was a Punjabi poet, writer, and playwright who was known for his contribution to Punjabi literature. He was a prominent voice of the Punjabi Renaissance and his works often addressed social issues. He passed away at a young age of 36 but his literary works continue to inspire and influence Punjabi culture.

166. Sukhdev Thapar: Sukhdev Thapar was an Indian revolutionary who actively participated in the

Indian independence movement. He was a member of the Hindustan Socialist Republican Association (HSRA) and was involved in the Lahore conspiracy case of 1930. He was executed by the

British along with Bhagat Singh and Shivaram Rajguru on 23 March 1931.

167. Surinder Kaur: Surinder Kaur was a prominent Punjabi folk singer who sang traditional Punjabi folk songs. She was known for her soulful and melodious voice and was popularly known as the "Nightingale of Punjab." Her music continues to be popular even today and has inspired generations of Punjabi singers.

168. Tara Singh Vaid: Tara Singh Vaid was an Indian independence activist and a member of the Indian National Congress. He actively participated in the Quit India Movement and was imprisoned by the British. After India's independence, he served as a member of the Lok Sabha and was appointed as the governor of Orissa.

169. Tarlochan Singh: Tarlochan Singh was an Indian politician and a member of the Indian National Congress. He was actively involved in the Indian independence movement and served as a member of the Punjab Legislative Assembly. He also served as a member of the Rajya Sabha and the Lok Sabha.

170. Teja Singh Samundri: Teja Singh Samundri was an Indian freedom fighter and a member of the Indian National Congress. He actively participated in the Indian independence movement and was imprisoned by the British. He later served as the President of the Shiromani Gurdwara Prabandhak Committee (SGPC) and worked towards.

171. Bhai Parmanand : Bhai Parmanand was an Indian nationalist, freedom fighter, and leader of the Ghadar Party, a revolutionary organization that sought to overthrow British rule in India. He was also a prolific writer and editor, and his writings and speeches inspired many to join the struggle for independence.

172. Bhikaiji Cama : Bhikaiji Cama was an Indian independence activist who is best known for designing the Indian national flag. She was also a writer and speaker, and she worked closely with other Indian nationalist leaders like Dadabhai Naoroji and Shyamji Krishnavarma to

promote the cause of Indian independence in Europe and the United States.

173. C. Rajagopalachari C. Rajagopalachari, also known as Rajaji, was an Indian independence activist, politician, and writer who played a key role in the Indian National Congress and the Indian freedom struggle. He was a close associate of Mahatma Gandhi and served as the first Indian GovernorGeneral of independent India.

174. Chittaranjan Das Chittaranjan Das, also known as Deshbandhu, was an Indian independence activist, lawyer, and politician who played a key role in the Indian National Congress and the freedom struggle. He was a close associate of Mahatma Gandhi and was known for his passionate speeches and writings in support of Indian independence.

175. Giani Zail Singh Giani Zail Singh was an Indian politician who served as the seventh President of India from 1982 to 1987. Before becoming President, he was a freedom fighter and leader of the Indian National Congress. He also served as the Chief Minister of Punjab and as a member of Parliament.

176. Gopal Krishna Gokhale Gopal Krishna Gokhale was an Indian political leader and social reformer who played an important role in the Indian independence movement. He was a mentor to Mahatma Gandhi and helped shape his political philosophy. He was also a member of the Indian National Congress and served as its president in 1905.

177. Hargobind Khorana Hargobind Khorana was an Indian-American biochemist who won the Nobel Prize in Physiology or Medicine in 1968. He was born in India and later emigrated to the United States, where he worked on the genetic code and helped lay the foundation for modern molecular biology. His work had a profound impact on medicine and biotechnology.

178. Jawaharlal Nehru Jawaharlal Nehru was an Indian politician and statesman who played a key role in the Indian independence

movement and later became the first Prime Minister of independent India. He was a close associate of Mahatma Gandhi and served as the President of the Indian National Congress several times.

179. Jivatram Kripalani Jivatram Kripalani was an Indian politician and independence activist who played a key role in the Indian National Congress and the freedom struggle. He was a close associate of Mahatma Gandhi and served as the President of the Congress Party in the 1940s. He later founded the Kisan Mazdoor Praja Party and was a member of Parliament.

180. Bhim Sen Sachar: A lawyer, judge, and human rights activist who was a member of the Constituent Assembly of India and served as the Chief Justice of the Delhi High Court.

181. Darshan Singh Canadian: A Canadian Sikh leader who advocated for Sikh sovereignty and independence.

182. Giani Kartar Singh: A Sikh scholar and theologian who served as the Jathedar (head) of Akal Takht, one of the five seats of temporal authority for Sikhs.

183. Gurbaksh Singh Kala Afghana: A Sikh scholar and writer who was known for his controversial views on Sikhism and the role of religion in society.

184. Gurbaksh Singh Khalsa: A Sikh activist who went on hunger strike in 2013 to demand the release of Sikh prisoners who had completed their sentences.

185. Harkishan Singh Surjeet: A Communist leader who served as the General Secretary of the Communist Party of India (Marxist) and played a significant role in Indian politics.

186. Harmandir Singh: A Sikh activist and journalist who was a vocal critic of the Indian government's treatment of Sikhs.

187. Harpartap Singh Bajwa: A Sikh activist who was involved in the movement for Khalistan, a proposed independent Sikh state.

188. Jaswant Singh Khalra: A human rights activist who exposed the Punjab Police's role in the extrajudicial killings of thousands of Sikhs during the 1980s and 1990s.

189. Joginder Singh Sahnan: A Sikh activist who was involved in the Khalistan movement and was assassinated in 1994.

190. Kirpal Singh was a spiritual leader and founder of the Kirpal Ashram. He preached the message of love and peace throughout his life.

191. Kishori Lal was a freedom fighter who played an active role in the Quit India Movement. He was imprisoned for several years for his involvement in the struggle for independence.

192. M. S. Randhawa was a distinguished civil servant and the first Indian to be appointed as the Director-General of Tourism. He also served as the Governor of several states in India.

193. Madan Lal Dhingra was a revolutionary who assassinated Sir William Hutt Curzon Wyllie, a British official in London in 1909. He was subsequently executed for his actions.

194. Manmohan Singh was the Prime Minister of India from 2004 to 2014. He is widely regarded as an economist and played a key role in shaping India's economic policies during his tenure.

195. Mehr Chand Mahajan was a prominent lawyer and politician who served as the Chief Justice of India and the Prime Minister of Jammu and Kashmir.

196 . Mirza Ghulam Ahmad was a religious leader who founded the Ahmadiyya movement in the late 19th century.

197. Mohan Singh Deb was a revolutionary who played an active role in the Indian independence movement. He was a member of the Indian National Army (INA) and fought against the British during World War II.

198 . Navjot Singh Sidhu is a former Indian cricketer and politician who played an important role in the Indian cricket team's success

during the 1990s. He later became a Member of Parliament and served as a Minister in the Punjab government.

199. Pritam Singh Dhillon was a freedom fighter who participated in the Indian independence movement and was imprisoned by the British authorities for his involvement.

200. Raja Mahendra Pratap was a freedom fighter and a member of the Indian National Congress. He played an active role in the Non-Cooperation Movement and was later exiled to Europe by the British authorities.

201. Ranjit Singh was the founder of the Sikh Empire and ruled over Punjab in the early 19th century.

202. Sahir Ludhianvi was a renowned poet and lyricist who wrote many famous songs and poems in Hindi and Urdu.

203. Sarojini Naidu was a poet and politician who played an active role in the Indian independence movement. She was the first Indian woman to become the President of the Indian National Congress.

204. Satyendra Nath Bose was a physicist and mathematician who made significant contributions to the development of quantum mechanics.

205. Sohan Singh Bhakna was a freedom fighter and a founding member of the Ghadar Party, which played an important role in the Indian independence movement.

206 . Sushil Kumar Sahu was a revolutionary who played an active role in the Indian independence movement. He was a member of the Indian National Army (INA) and fought against the British during World War II.

207. Thakur Das Bhargava was a freedom fighter and a member of the Indian National Congress. He played an active role in the Quit India Movement and was imprisoned by the British authorities.

208 . V. P. Menon was a civil servant who played an important role in India's independence movement. He was the Constitutional Advisor

to the last Viceroy of India and played a key role in the integration of the princely states into India.

209. Vinayak Damodar Savarkar was a revolutionary and a political leader who played an important role in the Indian independence movement. He was also the founder of the Hindutva movement.

210. Virendranath Chattopadhyaya was a revolutionary who played an active role in the Indian independence movement. He was a member of the Indian National Congress and later became a Marxist.

211. Vishnu Ganesh Pingle was a revolutionary who played an active role in the Indian independence movement.

Chapter Six: World War and Punjabi Soldiers

During both World War I and World War II, Punjabi soldiers played a significant role in the British Indian Army. Punjabis made up a large proportion of the British Indian Army, and their contributions were crucial to the success of the British Empire's military campaigns.

In World War I, over 400,000 Indian soldiers served in the British Indian Army, with more than 100,000 of them being Punjabi soldiers. Punjabi soldiers fought in major battles such as the Battle of Neuve Chapelle, the Battle of Loos, and the Battle of Ypres. They also served in several theaters of war, including Mesopotamia, East Africa, and Gallipoli.

In World War II, over 2.5 million Indian soldiers served in the British Indian Army, with Punjabis making up a significant portion of this number. Punjabi soldiers played a crucial role in several major battles, including the Battle of El Alamein, the Battle of Monte Cassino, and the Burma Campaign. Punjabi soldiers also served in other theaters of war, including North Africa, Italy, and Southeast Asia.

Despite their contributions to the British war effort, Punjabi soldiers faced discrimination and prejudice from their British commanders. They were often paid less than their British counterparts and were not given the same opportunities for advancement. However, Punjabi soldiers remained loyal to the British Empire and continued to serve in the army until India gained independence in 1947.

After India's independence, many Punjabi soldiers chose to continue their military service in the newly formed Indian Army. Today, Punjabis continue to make up a significant portion of the Indian Army and have served in several conflicts, including the Indo-Pakistani Wars and the Kargil War. The contributions of Punjabi soldiers during the World Wars remain an important part of their military history and cultural heritage.

6.1 The Roles of punjabi warriors in war

The Punjabi soldiers played a significant role in both World War I and World War II, fighting for the British Empire. During this time, many Punjabi soldiers were recruited into the British Indian Army, which was the main force that the British Empire relied on for military support in the region.

One of the main reasons why Punjabi soldiers joined the war effort was a sense of duty and loyalty to the British Empire. They saw it as their responsibility to serve their country and defend their empire against enemies.

Another reason why Punjabi soldiers joined the war effort was for economic incentives. Many soldiers came from impoverished backgrounds and saw the army as a way to earn a steady income and provide for their families.

Despite their willingness to serve, Punjabi soldiers faced many challenges during their time in the army. One of the biggest obstacles was the language barrier. Many Punjabi soldiers did not speak English, which made it difficult for them to communicate with their British officers.

Discrimination was also a common problem faced by Punjabi soldiers. They were often treated as second-class citizens and were denied equal opportunities for promotions and recognition.

Despite these challenges, Punjabi soldiers played a critical role in some of the most important battles and campaigns of the World Wars. In World War I, Punjabi soldiers fought in the Battle of Neuve Chapelle, the Battle of Ypres, and the Battle of the Somme. In World War II, Punjabi soldiers fought in the Burma Campaign and the North African Campaign.

One of the most notable contributions of Punjabi soldiers during the World Wars was their bravery and sacrifice. Many soldiers showed remarkable courage in the face of adversity, and some even sacrificed their lives for their country and the British Empire.

For their bravery, Punjabi soldiers were often recognized with medals and honors. Some soldiers were awarded the Victoria Cross, which is the highest military decoration in the British Empire. Others were knighted by the British Crown for their service.

Overall, the role of Punjabi soldiers in the World Wars was an important chapter in the history of the Punjabi people. They demonstrated courage, resilience, and a deep commitment to their country and their empire, leaving behind a legacy that will be remembered for generations to come.

6.1.1 Joining the war

Joining the war effort during World War I and World War II was a significant decision for Punjabi warriors. Many Punjabi soldiers volunteered to join the British Indian Army and fight for the British Empire during these wars.

For some Punjabi soldiers, joining the army was seen as a way to earn a steady income and provide for their families. Many came from impoverished backgrounds and saw the army as a means to improve their economic situation.

For others, joining the army was a matter of duty and loyalty to the British Empire. Punjabi soldiers felt a sense of obligation to serve their country and defend their empire against its enemies.

Joining the army was not an easy decision, however. Punjabi soldiers faced many challenges during their time in the army, including discrimination and language barriers. Many soldiers did not speak English, which made it difficult for them to communicate with their British officers. Discrimination was also a common problem faced by Punjabi soldiers, who were often treated as second-class citizens and denied equal opportunities for promotions and recognition.

Despite these challenges, Punjabi soldiers remained dedicated to their cause and played a significant role in many important battles and campaigns. During World War I, Punjabi soldiers fought in some of the most critical battles, including the Battle of Neuve Chapelle, the Battle of Ypres, and the Battle of the Somme. In World War II, Punjabi soldiers fought in the Burma Campaign and the North African Campaign, among others.

Punjabi soldiers demonstrated remarkable bravery and courage during these wars, often facing harsh conditions and extreme danger. Many soldiers were recognized for their bravery and sacrifice with medals and honors, including the Victoria Cross, which is the highest military decoration in the British Empire.

Overall, the decision to join the war effort during World War I and World War II was a significant one for Punjabi warriors. Despite the challenges they faced, they remained dedicated to their cause and made significant contributions to the war effort, leaving behind a legacy that is still celebrated today.

1. Duty and loyalty to the British Empire were important motivating factors for Punjabi soldiers who joined the British Indian Army during World War I and World War II.

At the time, the British Empire controlled many parts of the world, including India, and Punjabi soldiers saw it as their duty to serve their country and defend their empire against its enemies. They felt a strong sense of obligation to contribute to the war effort and support their fellow soldiers.

Many Punjabi soldiers also felt a sense of loyalty to the British Empire. They saw it as their responsibility to protect their country and its interests, and they believed that joining the war effort was a way to demonstrate their loyalty and commitment.

For some Punjabi soldiers, loyalty to the British Empire was also linked to economic incentives. Many soldiers came from impoverished backgrounds and saw the army as a way to earn a steady income and improve their economic situation.

Despite the challenges they faced, including discrimination and language barriers, Punjabi soldiers remained dedicated to their cause and committed to serving their country and the British Empire. They played a significant role in many important battles and campaigns, demonstrating remarkable bravery and sacrifice.

Overall, duty and loyalty to the British Empire were important motivating factors for Punjabi soldiers during World War I and World War II. They saw it as their responsibility to serve their country and defend their empire, and they remained committed to their cause despite the challenges they faced.

2. *Economic incentives* played a role in motivating some Punjabi soldiers to join the British Indian Army during World War I and World War II.

Many Punjabi soldiers came from impoverished backgrounds and saw the army as a way to earn a steady income and improve their economic situation. Joining the army meant that they would receive a regular salary, which was often higher than what they would earn in other professions.

In addition to their salary, soldiers also received other benefits, such as free healthcare, education, and housing. These benefits were especially attractive to soldiers who came from poor families and lacked access to basic necessities.

For some Punjabi soldiers, economic incentives were not the only motivating factor for joining the army.

They also saw it as a way to serve their country and demonstrate their loyalty to the British Empire. However, for many soldiers, the economic benefits were an important consideration in their decision to join the army.

Despite the economic incentives, serving in the army was not an easy job, and soldiers faced many challenges, including discrimination and language barriers. However, Punjabi soldiers remained dedicated to their cause and committed to serving their country and the British Empire, even in the face of adversity.

3. Punjabi soldiers faced ***several challenges*** during their time in the army, including discrimination and language barriers.

One of the significant challenges that Punjabi soldiers faced was discrimination. They were often treated as second-class citizens and denied equal opportunities for promotions and recognition. Many British officers held prejudiced views towards Indian soldiers and believed that they were not as competent as their British counterparts. This attitude resulted in Indian soldiers being assigned to less desirable roles, such as support staff or laborers.

Another significant challenge that Punjabi soldiers faced was the language barrier. Many soldiers did not speak English, which made it difficult for them to communicate with their British officers and understand orders. This often led to misunderstandings and mistakes, which could have dire consequences on the battlefield.

Punjabi soldiers also faced other challenges, such as harsh living conditions, disease, and lack of adequate training and equipment. Many soldiers were sent to fight in unfamiliar terrain and weather conditions, which could be extremely challenging.

Despite these challenges, Punjabi soldiers remained dedicated to their cause and committed to serving their country and the British Empire. They played a significant role in many important battles and campaigns, demonstrating remarkable bravery and sacrifice. Over time, their contributions helped to break down some of the discriminatory barriers that they faced in the army and paved the way for greater recognition and respect for Indian soldiers.

4. *Discrimination* was a common problem faced by Punjabi soldiers in the British Indian Army during World War I and World War II.

Punjabi soldiers were often discriminated against due to their race, ethnicity, and religion. They were treated as second-class citizens and denied equal opportunities for promotions and recognition. Many British officers held prejudiced views towards Indian soldiers and believed that they were not as competent as their British counterparts. This attitude resulted in Indian soldiers being assigned to less desirable roles, such as support staff or laborers.

Punjabi soldiers also faced discrimination based on their religion. Many Sikh soldiers, for example, were required to cut their hair and remove their turbans, which were important symbols of their faith. This was seen as a form of cultural and religious erasure, and it caused a great deal of tension and resentment among Sikh soldiers.

Despite the discrimination they faced, Punjabi soldiers remained dedicated to their cause and committed to serving their country and the British Empire. They played a significant role in many important battles and campaigns, demonstrating remarkable bravery and sacrifice. Over time, their contributions helped to break down some of the discriminatory barriers that they faced in the army and paved the way for greater recognition

6.2 key battles and campaigns

Punjabi soldiers played a significant role in many key battles and campaigns during World War I and World War II. Here are some examples:

World War I:

1. Battle of Neuve Chapelle: In March 1915, Punjabi soldiers fought alongside British troops in the Battle of Neuve Chapelle in France. They played a critical role in capturing the German-held village of Neuve Chapelle, which was a major strategic victory for the Allies.
2. Battle of Gallipoli: Punjabi soldiers also fought in the ill-fated Gallipoli Campaign in Turkey in 1915. They faced challenging terrain and harsh weather conditions, but their bravery and determination helped to secure several key victories.
3. Battle of the Somme: In July 1916, Punjabi soldiers fought in the Battle of the Somme in France, one of the deadliest battles of World War I. They were instrumental in capturing key German positions, and their bravery and sacrifice were widely praised.

World War II:

1. Battle of El Alamein: Punjabi soldiers played a critical role in the Battle of El Alamein in North Africa in 1942. They helped to secure a decisive victory for the Allies, which marked a turning point in the war in North Africa.
2. Battle of Monte Cassino: In 1944, Punjabi soldiers fought alongside British and Commonwealth troops in the Battle of Monte Cassino in Italy. They played a significant role in

capturing the strategic hilltop monastery of Monte Cassino, which had been a major German stronghold.

3. Battle of Kohima: Punjabi soldiers also fought in the Battle of Kohima in northeastern India in 1944. They faced intense fighting against Japanese troops, but their bravery and determination helped to secure a key victory for the Allies.

6.2.1 Other Battles

Punjabi soldiers played a crucial role in many key battles and campaigns during World War I and World War II. Here are some additional examples:

World War I:

1. Battle of Ypres: In April 1915, Punjabi soldiers fought in the Battle of Ypres in Belgium, one of the first major battles of the war. They faced heavy German bombardment and gas attacks, but their bravery and determination helped to hold the line against the enemy.
2. Battle of Loos: In September 1915, Punjabi soldiers fought in the Battle of Loos in France, a major offensive launched by the Allies. They faced heavy casualties, but their bravery and sacrifice helped to secure some key victories.
3. Battle of Cambrai: In November 1917, Punjabi soldiers fought in the Battle of Cambrai in France, one of the first battles in which tanks were used on a large scale. They played a critical role in capturing several key German positions, which helped to turn the tide of the battle.

World War II:

1. Siege of Tobruk: In 1941, Punjabi soldiers fought in the Siege of Tobruk in North Africa, a critical battle that helped to secure the Allies' hold on the region. They faced intense fighting and harsh desert conditions, but their bravery and determination helped to secure a crucial victory.
2. Battle of Imphal: In 1944, Punjabi soldiers fought in the Battle of Imphal in northeastern India, a major offensive launched by the Japanese. They faced fierce resistance from

the enemy, but their bravery and sacrifice helped to repel the attack and secure a key victory for the Allies.

3. Battle of the Arakan: In 1944, Punjabi soldiers fought in the Battle of the Arakan in western Burma, a critical campaign that helped to secure the Allies' hold on the region. They faced challenging terrain and fierce resistance from the Japanese, but their bravery and determination helped to secure some key victories.

6.2.2 *The Burma Campaign and the North African Campaign*

The Burma Campaign:

The Burma Campaign was fought in the jungles and mountainous regions of Burma (now Myanmar) between 1942 and 1945. The campaign was fought between the Allied forces, led by the British, and the

Japanese. Punjabi soldiers played a critical role in this campaign, fighting alongside other Commonwealth soldiers and Indian Army troops.

The campaign was particularly challenging due to the harsh terrain and weather conditions, as well as the fierce resistance put up by the Japanese. The Punjabi soldiers fought in many key battles, including the Battle of Imphal and the Battle of Kohima. They faced intense fighting and challenging conditions, but their bravery and determination helped to secure several key victories for the Allies.

The North African Campaign:

The North African Campaign was fought in the deserts of North Africa between 1940 and 1943. The campaign was fought between the Allied forces, led by the British, and the Axis powers, led by Germany and Italy. Punjabi soldiers played a critical role in this campaign, fighting alongside soldiers from other Commonwealth countries and Indian Army troops.

The campaign was particularly challenging due to the harsh desert conditions and the strength of the Axis forces. The Punjabi soldiers fought in many key battles, including the Battle of El Alamein and the Siege of Tobruk. They faced intense fighting and challenging conditions, but their bravery and determination helped to secure several key victories for the Allies.

Overall, the Burma Campaign and the North African Campaign were two significant campaigns of World War II in which Punjabi soldiers played a crucial role. Their bravery, sacrifice, and dedication to their cause helped to secure many important victories for the Allied forces and contributed to the ultimate defeat of the Axis powers.

6.3 The bravery and sacrifices

The bravery and sacrifices of Punjabi soldiers in both World War I and World War II cannot be overstated.

Despite facing discrimination and other challenges, these soldiers fought with great courage and determination, often in some of the toughest battles and campaigns of the wars.

Punjabi soldiers were known for their fierce fighting skills and their ability to withstand difficult conditions. They fought in some of the harshest environments, including the jungles and mountains of Burma, the deserts of North Africa, and the trenches of the Western Front. They faced not only enemy fire but also diseases, extreme weather, and other hazards.

Many Punjabi soldiers also made great sacrifices for their country and their fellow soldiers. They often had to leave behind their families and loved ones to go to war, and many never returned home. In World War I, more than 74,000 Indian soldiers were killed, and in World War II, more than 87,000 Indian soldiers lost their lives.

Despite the risks, Punjabi soldiers continued to fight with great courage and determination. They earned a reputation for being some of the bravest soldiers on the battlefield, often charging into enemy fire without hesitation. Many earned honors and medals for their bravery, including the Victoria Cross, the highest military decoration awarded for valor in the face of the enemy.

Overall, the bravery and sacrifices of Punjabi soldiers in World War I and World War II played a critical role in the Allied victory. Their dedication and heroism will never be forgotten, and they will always be remembered as true legends of the wars.

6.3.1 Recognition Awarded

During the World Wars, Punjabi soldiers were typically not given the same level of recognition as soldiers from other parts of the British Empire, such as the UK, Australia, and New Zealand. Despite the fact that they made up a significant proportion of the British Indian Army, they were often overlooked in favor of soldiers from other parts of the Empire.

However, many Punjabi soldiers did receive recognition for their service and bravery. Over 4,000 Indian soldiers were awarded the Victoria Cross, the highest military decoration for valor in the face of the enemy. Many others received other honors and medals for their service, including the Indian Order of Merit and the Distinguished Service Order.

After the wars, the contribution of Punjabi soldiers to the Allied victory was more widely recognized. In India, they were celebrated as heroes and remembered for their bravery and sacrifice. Monuments and memorials were erected in their honor, and their stories were preserved in books and films.

In the UK, the contribution of Punjabi soldiers was also recognized, although not to the same extent as soldiers from the UK and other parts of the Empire. In recent years, efforts have been made to rectify this, with more recognition and commemoration of the role that Punjabi soldiers played in the World Wars. For example, in 2018, a statue was unveiled in Smethwick, UK, to commemorate the contribution of Sikh soldiers in the wars.

Overall, while Punjabi soldiers did not always receive the recognition they deserved during the wars, their contribution has been increasingly recognized in the years since, both in India and around the world.

6.4 Contributions In History

The contributions of Punjabi soldiers to history cannot be overstated. They played a significant role in both World War I and World War II, fighting with great bravery and determination in some of the most difficult battles and campaigns of the wars.

Punjabi soldiers also made important contributions to the history of India and the wider world. Their service in the British Indian Army helped to shape the history of India during the colonial period, and their sacrifices played a critical role in the eventual independence of India.

Furthermore, the bravery and sacrifice of Punjabi soldiers helped to change attitudes towards India and its people in the UK and around the world. Their service challenged stereotypes and prejudices, and helped to pave the way for greater recognition and respect for Indian people and culture.

In addition, the contributions of Punjabi soldiers helped to shape the history of the British Empire and the wider world. Their service in the World Wars, alongside soldiers from other parts of the Empire, helped to secure the Allied victory and shape the course of 20th-century history.

Overall, the contributions of Punjabi soldiers to history are significant and far-reaching, and their bravery and sacrifice will be remembered for generations to come.

6.4.1 World war 1: Notable Soldiers

1. Sepoy Khudadad Khan: Khan was the first Indian soldier to receive the Victoria Cross, the highest award for bravery in the British Empire. He earned this honor during the First Battle of Ypres in

1914, when he continued to man a machine-gun after his comrades had been killed or wounded.

1. Naik Darwan Singh Negi: Negi was a soldier from the Garhwal Rifles, which was part of the British Indian Army. During the Battle of Neuve Chapelle in 1915, he was responsible for capturing a German machine-gun post, and he later led his men in the capture of a second position.
2. Subedar Gobind Singh: Singh was a soldier from the Sikh Regiment who earned the Military Cross for his bravery during the Battle of Loos in 1915. He led a charge against a German machine-gun post, and his actions allowed his unit to capture their objective.
3. Rifleman Gabar Singh Negi: Negi was a soldier from the Garhwal Rifles who earned the Victoria Cross during the Battle of Festubert in 1915. He charged a German machine-gun post, and though he was wounded, he continued to attack until he was killed.
4. Risaldar Badlu Singh: Singh was a soldier from the 14th Murray's Jat Lancers who earned the Victoria Cross during the Battle of Cambrai in 1917. He led a charge against a German machinegun post, and he and his men captured the position, taking 50 prisoners in the process.
5. Naik Shahamad Khan: Khan was a soldier from the 129th Duke of Connaught's Own Baluchis who earned the Victoria

Cross during the Battle of Cambrai in 1917. He led a charge against a German machine-gun post, and he and his men captured the position and took several prisoners.

6. Jemadar Mir Dast: Dast was a soldier from the 55th Coke's Rifles (Frontier Force) who earned the Victoria Cross during the Battle of Cambrai in 1917. He led a charge against a German machinegun post, and he and his men captured the position and took several prisoners.

7. Lance Naik Karam Singh: Singh was a soldier from the Sikh Regiment who earned the Victoria Cross during the Battle of the Lys in 1918. He led a charge against a German machine-gun post, and he and his men captured the position and took several prisoners.

6.4.2 World War 2 : Notable Soldiers

1. Subedar Joginder Singh: Singh was a Punjabi soldier who served in the British Indian Army. During the Battle of Saragarhi, he led a small unit of soldiers against a much larger force of Afghan tribesmen. Despite being vastly outnumbered, he and his men fought bravely to the end and were posthumously awarded the Indian Order of Merit.

2. Captain Gurbachan Singh Salaria: Salaria was a Punjabi soldier who served in the Indian Army.During the Congo Crisis in 1961, he volunteered to lead a dangerous mission to rescue UN hostages. He was killed in action during the mission, and was posthumously awarded the Param Vir Chakra, India's highest military honor.

3. Naik Gian Singh: Singh was a Punjabi soldier who served in the British Indian Army. During the Battle of Gazala in 1942, he led an attack on enemy positions despite being seriously wounded. He was posthumously awarded the Victoria Cross for his bravery.

4. Subedar Major Bana Singh: Singh was a Punjabi soldier who served in the Indian Army. During the Siachen Conflict in 1987, he led a small unit of soldiers in a daring attack on a heavily fortified enemy position. His unit was vastly outnumbered, but they fought bravely and succeeded in capturing the position. Singh was awarded the Param Vir Chakra for his bravery.

5. Lance Naik Karam Singh: Singh was a Punjabi soldier who served in the British Indian Army. During the Battle of Sangro in 1943, he led an attack on enemy positions despite being seriously wounded.He was posthumously awarded the Victoria Cross for his bravery.

6. Naik Jadunath Singh: Singh was a Punjabi soldier who served

in the British Indian Army. During the Battle of Chushul in 1962, he led his men in a daring attack on a heavily fortified enemy position.His unit was vastly outnumbered, but they fought bravely and succeeded in capturing the position.Singh was posthumously awarded the Param Vir Chakra for his bravery.

7. Lieutenant Colonel Tarapore: Tarapore was a Punjabi soldier who served in the Indian Army. During the Indo-Pakistani War of 1965, he led his unit in a series of successful attacks on enemy positions. He was killed in action during the Battle of Chawinda, but his leadership and bravery inspired his men to continue the fight.

8. Captain Fateh Singh: Singh was a Punjabi soldier who served in the Indian Army. During the Indo-Pakistani War of 1971, he led a small unit of soldiers in a daring attack on enemy positions. His unit was vastly outnumbered, but they fought bravely and succeeded in capturing the position. Singh was awarded the Maha Vir Chakra for his bravery.

Chapter Seven : Modern-day Warriors

After the partition of India in 1947, Punjabi warriors made significant contributions to their respective countries. Here are some of their noteworthy contributions:

1. Service in the Armed Forces: Many Punjabi soldiers served in the Indian and Pakistani armies after independence. The Punjabi regiment of the Indian Army and the Punjab Regiment of the Pakistani Army are two of the most respected and prestigious units of their respective armies. Punjabi soldiers have participated in numerous conflicts and wars, including the Indo-Pakistani wars of 1947, 1965, and 1971, the Kargil War of 1999, and various other operations.

2. Bravery in Battle: Punjabi soldiers have exhibited great bravery and courage in the face of adversity. During the 1965 Indo-Pakistani War, the Battle of Asal Uttar saw the Indian Army's 4th Mountain Division, predominantly composed of Punjabi soldiers, successfully repel a major Pakistani offensive. Similarly, Pakistan's 1st Armoured Division, primarily composed of Punjabi soldiers, played a key role in the Battle of Chawinda.

3. Contributions to Sports: Punjabi wrestlers, known as "Pehlwans," are renowned for their strength and skill. Famous Punjabi wrestlers include Gama Pehlwan, who was undefeated in over 5,000 matches, and Dara Singh, who became a household name in India through his wrestling and acting careers. Punjabi boxers, such as Kaur Singh and Vijender Singh, have also made their mark in the world of sports by winning medals at international competitions.

4. Political Contributions: Punjabi political figures have played a significant role in shaping the history of India and Pakistan.

The first Indian Prime Minister, Jawaharlal Nehru, was a Punjabi, as was the first Pakistani Prime Minister, Liaquat Ali Khan. Other notable Punjabi political figures include Zulfikar Ali Bhutto and Manmohan Singh.

Overall, Punjabi warriors have continued to make significant contributions to various fields and aspects of society even after the partition of India in 1947. They remain an important and influential community in both India and Pakistan.

7.1 The Journey of punjabi warriors in Indian Army

The Punjabi community has had a significant role in the Indian Army, with Punjabi soldiers serving in the armed forces since the British colonial era. After the partition of India in 1947, Punjabi soldiers continued to play a crucial role in the Indian Army.

The Punjabi regiment of the Indian Army is one of the most decorated and respected units, with a long and illustrious history of service. Punjabi soldiers have participated in numerous conflicts and wars, including the Indo-Pakistani wars of 1947, 1965, and 1971, the Kargil War of 1999, and various other operations.

During the 1965 Indo-Pakistani War, the Battle of Asal Uttar saw the Indian Army's 4th Mountain Division, which was predominantly composed of Punjabi soldiers, successfully repel a major Pakistani offensive.

The division's success in this battle earned it the nickname "Chauthi Jalap" (Fourth Inferno).

Punjabi soldiers have also made significant contributions to peacekeeping operations in various parts of the world. Indian peacekeeping forces, including Punjabi soldiers, have served in places like Congo, Lebanon, and Cambodia, among others.

In addition to their military service, Punjabi soldiers have also made notable contributions to society. Many soldiers have been awarded medals and honors for their bravery and service, and some have gone on to become successful in other fields such as politics, sports, and business.

Overall, Punjabi soldiers have played a vital role in the defense of India and have demonstrated great bravery and courage in the face of adversity. They continue to be an integral part of the Indian Army and are held in high esteem by the people of India.

7.1.1 The Partition of India

The Partition of India was a traumatic event that forever changed the course of history for Punjabi soldiers and their families. Many Punjabi soldiers faced a difficult choice as the country was divided in 1947. They were forced to choose between serving in the Indian Army or the newly-formed Pakistani Army. The decision was not an easy one, as it meant leaving behind friends, family, and a way of life that they had known for generations.

One such soldier was Manjit Singh, a proud Punjabi who had served in the Indian Army for over a decade. As the news of the impending partition spread, Manjit found himself torn between his duty to the Indian Army and his loyalty to his homeland. He knew that whichever side he chose, he would be leaving behind loved ones and a way of life that he cherished.

Despite the uncertainty and fear that surrounded the partition, Manjit ultimately decided to remain in the

Indian Army. He believed that by serving his country, he could help protect his fellow Punjabis from the violence and chaos that was sure to come with the partition. It was a difficult decision, but one that he knew was the right one.

As the date of the partition drew nearer, tensions in the region escalated. Riots broke out, and violence became commonplace. Manjit's own village was not spared, and he watched in horror as homes were burned and families were torn apart.

Despite the chaos and heartache, Manjit remained committed to his duty. He knew that his fellow Punjabi soldiers were facing the same difficult decision that he had, and he took comfort in the fact that they were all united in their love for their homeland.

In the end, the partition of India had a profound impact on Punjabi soldiers and their families. It forced them to make difficult choices and endure unimaginable hardship, but it also showed their resilience and commitment to their country and their people. Manjit, and the many other Punjabi soldiers like him, stood firm in the face of adversity and proved that they were modern-day warriors, dedicated to protecting their homeland and their people.

7.1.2 Recruitment

Once upon a time, in the state of Punjab in India, there lived a young man named Raj who belonged to a humble farming family. Despite facing financial difficulties, Raj was determined to support his family and contribute to his country in any way possible.

One day, as he was walking down the street, Raj noticed a recruitment poster for the Indian Army. He had always been fascinated by the stories of bravery and sacrifice of soldiers and decided to explore this opportunity.

Raj went to the recruitment center and underwent rigorous physical and mental tests. Finally, he was selected to join the Indian Army as a soldier. His family was overjoyed, but also worried for his safety.

As Raj began his training, he realized that the army was much more than just physical fitness and discipline. He learned about the values of integrity, loyalty, and patriotism. He also met many other Punjabi men who, like him, had joined the army to serve their country and support their families.

Raj underwent extensive training in combat, weapons handling, and strategic planning. He also learned about the diverse cultures and traditions of India's different regions. Raj felt proud to be part of such a diverse and inclusive organization that respected and valued all its members.

Finally, the day arrived when Raj was deployed to the frontlines. He was nervous but also determined to defend his country and protect its citizens. Raj's training kicked in, and he showed immense courage and bravery in the face of danger. He fought alongside his fellow soldiers, many of whom were also Punjabi men, and successfully defended his country.

Years went by, and Raj continued to serve in the army, rising through the ranks due to his dedication and hard work. He was able to provide for his family and ensure a better future for them. He also felt proud of his contribution to his country's defense and the impact he had on people's lives.

In the end, Raj retired from the army, but his legacy lived on. His story inspired many young Punjabi men to join the Indian Army, not just for economic reasons, but also for a sense of duty and love for their country. Raj's sacrifice and dedication were a testament to the spirit of the Indian Army and the Punjabi community's commitment to serving their country.

7.1.3 Training

Deep in the heart of Punjab, a group of young men gathered at the military training center. They came from different backgrounds, but they shared a common goal: to serve their country as soldiers. As they began their training, they quickly realized that the path to becoming a soldier was not an easy one. They were put through grueling physical exercises that tested their strength and endurance. They had to run, climb, and crawl their way through obstacle courses, all while carrying heavy weights on their backs.

But the physical training was only the beginning. The soldiers also had to undergo mental training, learning how to think strategically, work as a team, and keep a cool head in high-pressure situations. The soldiers were put through various simulations and drills, preparing them for different combat scenarios. They learned how to use various weapons, including rifles, pistols, and grenades. They also learned how to navigate different terrains, from deserts to forests to mountains.

The training was intense, and many of the soldiers struggled to keep up. But the Punjabi soldiers were a determined bunch, driven by their love for their country and their families. They pushed themselves to their limits, and sometimes beyond, determined to become the best soldiers they could be.

As the weeks went by, the soldiers grew stronger, faster, and more skilled. They learned how to work together as a team, covering each other's backs in battle. They also learned about the importance of discipline, following orders, and staying focused even when the going got tough.

Finally, the day arrived when the soldiers were deemed ready for combat. They were deployed to various parts of the country, tasked with protecting their fellow citizens from harm. The training they had undergone proved invaluable, as they faced various challenges and overcame them with bravery and skill.

As the years went by, the Punjabi soldiers continued to serve their country with pride, honor, and dedication. They became a symbol of strength and resilience, an inspiration to all who knew them. And the rigorous training they had undergone remained a testament to their unwavering commitment to serving their country as soldiers.

7.1.4 Indo-Pakistani War of 1947

It was the year 1947 when India gained its independence from the British Empire, leading to the partition of the country into India and Pakistan. But the division of the country was not peaceful, as it sparked a war between the two nations.

Among the soldiers who fought in the war were many brave Punjabi men. They had trained rigorously for months, learning how to fight and defend their country. And now, as the war broke out, they were ready to put their training to the test.

The Punjabi soldiers were deployed to various parts of the country, including the border between India and Pakistan. There, they faced off against enemy soldiers, some of whom were former comrades in arms. But the Punjabi soldiers were undaunted, and they fought with fierce determination and bravery. The war was a brutal one, with casualties on both sides. But the Punjabi soldiers refused to back down. They fought with everything they had, using their training and their instincts to stay alive and protect their fellow soldiers.

In one particular battle, a group of Punjabi soldiers found themselves outnumbered and outgunned. But they refused to give up, even when all hope seemed lost. They fought with everything they had, using grenades, rifles, and sheer determination to hold off the enemy.

Despite the odds, the Punjabi soldiers emerged victorious in that battle. Their bravery and tenacity had paid off, and they had secured an important victory for their country.

As the war raged on, the Punjabi soldiers continued to fight with all their might. They faced many challenges and obstacles, but they never gave up. They remained determined to protect their country and their people, no matter what the cost.

Finally, after many long months of fighting, the war came to an end. The Punjabi soldiers had played a critical role in securing victory for India, and their bravery and sacrifice were honored by their fellow citizens.

The Indo-Pakistani War of 1947 had been a difficult and trying time for all involved. But the Punjabi soldiers had risen to the challenge, fighting with honor and valor to protect their country and their people. Their legacy lived on, inspiring future generations of soldiers to fight for their country with pride and dedication.

7.1.5 Battle of Asal Uttar

The year was 1965, and India and Pakistan were once again at war. The Pakistani Army had launched a major offensive into Indian territory, and it seemed that nothing could stop them.

But the Punjabi soldiers were not about to let their country fall without a fight. They rallied together, determined to repel the enemy advance and protect their homeland.

The battle that ensued became known as the Battle of Asal Uttar, and it would go down in history as one of the greatest victories for the Indian Army.

The Punjabi soldiers played a key role in the battle. They fought with all their might, using their training and their courage to hold off the enemy advance. They engaged in fierce hand-to-hand combat, using their bayonets and knives to fight off the heavily armed Pakistani soldiers.

As the battle raged on, the Punjabi soldiers refused to back down. They held their ground, even as the enemy forces continued to press forward. They fought with all their might, determined to protect their country and their people.

And then, something miraculous happened. The Pakistani forces, who had been advancing steadily up until that point, suddenly began to retreat. The Punjabi soldiers, sensing an opportunity, launched a counterattack.

The counterattack was swift and brutal, catching the Pakistani forces off guard. The Punjabi soldiers fought with ferocity and determination, driving the enemy back and reclaiming the territory they had lost.

By the time the battle was over, the Punjabi soldiers had emerged victorious. They had repelled a major Pakistani offensive, and had secured an important victory for their country.

The Battle of Asal Uttar would go down in history as a testament to the bravery and courage of the

Punjabi soldiers. They had fought with all their might, and had emerged victorious against all odds. Their legacy lived on, inspiring future generations of soldiers to fight for their country with pride and dedication. And their victory in the Battle of Asal Uttar would forever be remembered as a shining moment in the history of the Indian Army.

7.1.6 Kargil War

In the year 1999, tensions between India and Pakistan were high, and the situation along the Line of Control (LoC) in the Kargil sector was particularly volatile. It was during this time that the Indian Army discovered that Pakistani soldiers had infiltrated into Indian territory, occupying key positions on the heights overlooking the strategic highway that connected Srinagar with Leh.

The Indian Army launched a massive operation to flush out the infiltrators, and among the soldiers who participated in the operation were many brave Punjabi men. These soldiers were deployed to the highaltitude areas, where they faced harsh weather conditions, difficult terrain, and a determined enemy. The Punjabi soldiers fought with all their might, using their training and their courage to hold off the enemy advance. They engaged in fierce battles, facing enemy fire and dodging bullets as they advanced up the mountainside.

The Kargil War was a brutal and challenging conflict, but the Punjabi soldiers refused to back down.

They fought with all their might, determined to protect their country and their people.

In one particularly challenging battle, a group of Punjabi soldiers found themselves facing a heavily fortified enemy position. The enemy was well-armed and well-prepared, and it seemed that victory was out of reach.

But the Punjabi soldiers refused to give up. They fought with everything they had, using their training and their instincts to stay alive and protect their fellow soldiers. They employed innovative tactics to overcome the enemy position, and after a fierce battle, they emerged victorious.

Despite the challenges they faced, the Punjabi soldiers continued to fight with all their might. They faced many obstacles, but they never gave up. They remained determined to protect their country and their people, no matter what the cost.

In the end, the Indian Army was successful in flushing out the infiltrators and securing the Kargil sector. The Punjabi soldiers had played a critical role in this victory, and their bravery and sacrifice were honored by their fellow citizens.

The Kargil War had been a difficult and trying time for all involved. But the Punjabi soldiers had risen to the challenge, fighting with honor and valor to protect their country and their people. Their legacy lived on, inspiring future generations of soldiers to fight for their country with pride and dedication.

7.1.7 Peacekeeping Operations

Punjabi soldiers have a long and proud history of serving their country, both on the battlefield and in times of peace. One of the most important ways that they have contributed to global peace and security is through their participation in United Nations peacekeeping operations.

Over the years, Punjabi soldiers have been deployed to various parts of the world as part of UN peacekeeping missions. These missions have taken them to some of the most challenging and volatile regions of the world, where they have worked tirelessly to promote peace, stability, and security. In many cases, the Punjabi soldiers have faced significant challenges in these missions. They have had to navigate complex political situations, deal with hostile local populations, and operate in difficult and often dangerous environments.

Despite these challenges, the Punjabi soldiers have remained committed to their mission. They have worked tirelessly to build relationships with local communities, to provide humanitarian assistance to those in need, and to promote peace and security in some of the most challenging regions of the world. In one particularly challenging mission, a group of Punjabi soldiers were deployed to a war-torn region of Africa. The local population was deeply divided, and there was significant tension and violence between different ethnic groups.

The Punjabi soldiers worked tirelessly to build trust and understanding between these groups. They engaged in dialogue with local leaders, helped to establish safe zones for refugees, and provided humanitarian aid to those in need.

Despite the many challenges they faced, the Punjabi soldiers remained committed to their mission. They worked tirelessly to promote peace and security, and their efforts were eventually successful in helping to bring an end to the conflict.

In recognition of their service and sacrifice, the Punjabi soldiers were honored by the UN and by their home country. Their commitment to global peace and security remains an inspiration to all who serve in UN peacekeeping missions.

7.1.8 Medal of Honor

Throughout history, Punjabi soldiers have demonstrated their bravery and commitment to duty, earning recognition and accolades for their service. One of the most prestigious honors that a soldier can receive is the Medal of Honor, awarded for exceptional acts of valor and bravery in combat. Many Punjabi soldiers have been awarded the Medal of Honor for their heroism and service to their country. Their stories are a testament to the courage and dedication of these brave men.

In one particularly notable incident, a group of Punjabi soldiers were involved in a fierce battle against a heavily armed enemy force. The enemy had the advantage of superior firepower and positioning, and it seemed as though victory was out of reach.

Despite the odds, the Punjabi soldiers refused to back down. They fought with all their might, using their training and their courage to hold off the enemy advance.

In the midst of the battle, one Punjabi soldier, in particular, distinguished himself with exceptional bravery. He charged forward, taking out enemy positions with his rifle and grenade. He fought with ferocity and determination, inspiring his fellow soldiers to fight harder and refuse to back down. Despite being wounded multiple times, the soldier refused to give up. He continued to fight, taking out enemy positions and inspiring his fellow soldiers with his bravery and determination.

For his exceptional acts of valor and bravery, the Punjabi soldier was awarded the Medal of Honor, the highest award for valor that a soldier can receive.

This soldier's story is just one example of the bravery and dedication that Punjabi soldiers have demonstrated throughout history. Their commitment to their country and their fellow soldiers has earned them the respect and admiration of people around the world.

The legacy of the Punjabi soldiers who have received the Medal of Honor lives on, inspiring future generations of soldiers to serve their country with honor and courage. They are a testament to the power of bravery and dedication, and their stories will continue to inspire us for generations to come.

7.1.9 Contribution to society

Punjabi soldiers have made significant contributions to various fields and aspects of society beyond their military service. They have used their skills, knowledge, and experience to make a positive impact on the world around them, inspiring others to follow in their footsteps.

One area in which Punjabi soldiers have made significant contributions is in the field of sports. Many Punjabi soldiers have excelled in sports at both the national and international levels. Their dedication to physical fitness and discipline has helped them achieve success in sports such as wrestling, boxing, and hockey.

In addition to sports, Punjabi soldiers have also made contributions to the fields of education and healthcare. Many have worked as teachers, sharing their knowledge and experience with future generations. Others have worked in healthcare, providing medical care to people in need.

One particularly notable example is a Punjabi soldier who became a doctor after retiring from the military. He used his medical skills to provide healthcare to people in remote and underserved areas, where access to medical care is often limited.

Another area in which Punjabi soldiers have made contributions is in the field of arts and culture. Many have used their talents to create works of art, music, and literature that reflect the rich cultural heritage of the Punjab region.

One particularly notable example is a Punjabi soldier who became a renowned poet after retiring from the military. His poems have inspired generations of people, capturing the beauty and complexity of the human experience.

These are just a few examples of the many ways in which Punjabi soldiers have made significant contributions to society beyond their military service. Their dedication to excellence and their commitment to making a positive impact on the world around them is a testament to the strength and resilience of the human spirit.

> In conclusion

As the final battle came to an end, the Punjabi warriors emerged victorious, their strength and courage forever etched in the annals of history. They had faced seemingly insurmountable challenges and overcome them with unwavering determination and a deep sense of duty.

As they stood amidst the rubble of the battlefield, the warriors looked back on the journey that had brought them to this moment. They had come from all walks of life, but had united under a common banner to fight for their country and their people.

Now, with the war won, they knew that their legacy would live on for generations to come. Their deeds would inspire others to follow in their footsteps, to fight for what was right and just, and to stand up against tyranny and oppression.

As they returned home, the warriors were greeted with cheers and celebrations. The people hailed them as heroes, thanking them for their sacrifices and their unwavering commitment to their country.

For the Punjabi warriors, this was more than just a victory in battle. It was a triumph of the human spirit, a testament to the power of courage, strength, and unity. They had proven that in the face of adversity, anything was possible, and that the legends of their bravery and heroism would endure for all time. And so, the Punjabi warriors continued on their journey, ready to face whatever challenges lay ahead. For they knew that no matter what came their way, they would always be guided by the legacy of their forefathers, the legends of the Punjabi warriors.

[1]A First Edition Book By Roman Sidhu

---

[1]Publish By SARDARGARH INC.
Exclusively on Google play books

Did you love *The Legends Of Punjabi Warriors*? Then you should read *The Secret Language Of Women*[1] by Roman Sidhu!

[2]

Unlock the Enigma of Female Communication

Dive into the mesmerizing realm of female communication in "The Secret Language of Women" and unearth the concealed meanings beneath their words and deeds. This guide unravels the intricate fabric of how women convey their thoughts, emotions, and desires through language, gestures, and unspoken cues.

Acquire profound insights into the art of deciphering their subtle signals, empowering you to forge deeper connections, navigate relationships with assurance, and bridge the chasms of comprehension. Whether you're a partner, confidant, or simply captivated by the

---

1. https://books2read.com/u/4A2PPK

2. https://books2read.com/u/4A2PPK

intricacies of human interaction, this ebook equips you with indispensable tools to unlock the secret language of women.

Within these pages, you'll discover:

- A journey into the myriad ways women express themselves and the reasons behind their expressions.

- Real-life anecdotes and case studies that illuminate the nuances of female communication.

- Pragmatic guidance on interpreting their words and actions with empathy and perspicacity.

- Strategies to enrich communication, cultivate trust, and fortify relationships.

"The Secret Language of Women" transcends mere words; it offers a profound glimpse into the elaborate tapestry of female expression. Decode the cipher, nurture meaningful bonds, and embark on a voyage toward a deeper understanding of the women in your life.

Also by Roman Sidhu

The Legends Of Punjabi Warriors
The Secret Language Of Women